Circuit Hikes in Harriman

*35 Loop Hikes and Trail Runs
in Harriman and Bear Mountain State Parks*

Don Weise

Edited by Daniel Chazin

2015
New York-New Jersey Trail Conference

Library of Congress Cataloging-in-Publication Data

Weise, Donald.
    Circuit hikes in Harriman : 35 loop hikes and trail runs in Harriman and
       Bear Mountain State Parks / Don Weise ; edited by Daniel Chazin.
    pages cm
    Includes index.
    ISBN 978-1-880775-93-6 (Paperback : alk. paper) --
    ISBN 978-1-880775-94-3 (eBook)
    1. Hiking--New York (State)--Harriman State Park--Guidebooks. 2. Hiking--New
York (State)--Bear Mountain State Park--Guidebooks. 3. Trails--New York (State)--
Harriman State Park--Guidebooks. 4. Trails--New York (State)--Bear Mountain State
Park--Guidebooks. 5. Harriman State Park (N.Y.)--Guidebooks. 6. Bear Mountain State
Park (N.Y.)--Guidebooks. I. Chazin, Daniel D. II. Title.
  GV199.42.N652H378 2015
  796.5109747--dc23
                      2015000177

Published by:
New York-New Jersey Trail Conference
600 Ramapo Valley Road
Mahwah, NJ 07430

Cartography: Allison Werberg and Jeremy Apgar
Photos: Daniel Chazin (except as otherwise indicated)
Cover photograph: *Hudson Valley from Bald Mountain* by Nick Zungoli
Book design, layout, and typography: Blair Saldanah [www.saldanah.com]
Body text set in Minion Pro Medium, 10/13
Headings set in Trade Gothic Bold Condensed No. 20
Printed by Versa Press, Inc., East Peoria, IL

TABLE OF CONTENTS

Introduction

As a hiker and hike leader, I love discovering and sharing trail lands with people, especially places as beautiful as Harriman-Bear Mountain State Parks. Its 52,000 acres of forested mountains, abundant lakes, wetlands, unique rock formations and mysterious mines await your discovery – a hiker's paradise of hidden gems and rich history.

For several decades, I have felt that Harriman needed (and deserved) its own comprehensive guidebook of carefully planned circuit hikes. Circuit (loop) hikes offer many advantages, including eliminating the need to set up car shuttles with others or retrace one's steps. When I first proposed this book to long-time Trail Conference volunteer Daniel Chazin, he enthusiastically supported the idea and offered to serve as the editor of the book. Daniel related to me that, when he edited Bill Myles' *Harriman Trails* book over 20 years ago, he had suggested including circuit hikes, but Bill declined to do so.

To provide maximum flexibility in planning hikes, I have included longer and shorter loop options in most chapters. In every chapter, you will find route maps, elevation profiles, distances and difficulty ratings to maximize your safety and enjoyment. To accommodate those who love trail running, cross-country skiing and walks on easier terrain, I have included eight additional chapters, which follow wider and more forgiving trails. Among these is the Horn Hill Bike Path loop, the only trail approved for mountain biking in Harriman.

Please note that five important park roads – Arden Valley Road, Route 106 (Kanawauke Road), Tiorati Brook Road, Lake Welch Drive and Perkins Memorial Drive – are normally closed to vehicular traffic in the winter. As a result, the trailheads for the hikes in Chapters 10 (Parker Cabin Mountain), 12 (Boston Mine and Stahahe High Peak), 21 (Pingyp Mountain) and 30 (Island Pond) may not be accessible during winter months.

I would like to thank all the dedicated volunteers who have contributed to this book. Special thanks go to my editor, Daniel Chazin, who contributed not only a wealth of experience but also considerable time to make this book the best it could be. In addition, Daniel contributed most of the photos and the index for the book. Bob Fuller managed to juggle his day job and volunteer positions as trail supervisor and maintainer as he diligently field-checked all of the hikes, with help from Marci Layton. I want to thank Dan Balogh for contributing many of his magnificent photos of Harriman to the book. Thanks also to the trail-running community, including Todd Jennings, who helped with the trail-run and ski chapters. Special thanks go to all volunteers and supporters of the New York-New Jersey Trail Conference. The Trail Conference builds, maintains and protects over 2,100 miles of trails, including nearly every marked trail described in this book. Enjoy your exploration of Harriman!

Don Weise

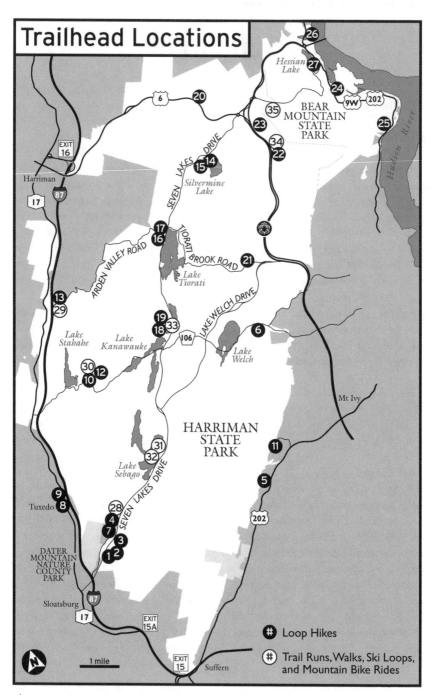

Trailhead Locations

Harriman
Sloatsburg
Suffern
Tuxedo

Hessian Lake
BEAR MOUNTAIN STATE PARK
Silvermine Lake
Lake Tiorati
Lake Stahahe
Lake Kanawauke
Lake Welch
Lake Sebago
HARRIMAN STATE PARK
DATER MOUNTAIN NATURE COUNTY PARK
Mt Ivy

SEVEN LAKES DRIVE
ARDEN VALLEY ROAD
TIORATI BROOK ROAD
LAKE WELCH DRIVE

Loop Hikes

Trail Runs, Walks, Ski Loops, and Mountain Bike Rides

1 mile

Legend for Hike Maps

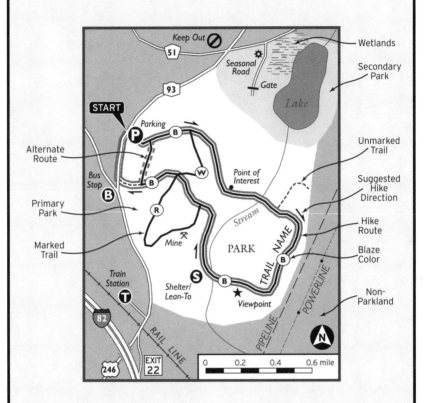

This map illustrates some of the important components of the hike maps contained in this book. A large START icon shows the beginning of the hike, the described route of a hike is highlighted on the map, and small arrows indicate the suggested hike direction.

Trail Blaze Colors

(B) Blue (Bl) Black (O) Orange (R) Red (W) White (Y) Yellow

(A) Appalachian Trail (white)

(L) Long Path (aqua)

Chapter 1 Ramapo Torne

Rating:	**Moderate to strenuous**
Distance:	**5.1 miles**
Hiking Time:	**3 hours**
Attractions:	**Panoramic views from Ramapo Torne and Torne View**
Lowest Elevation:	**440 feet**
Highest Elevation:	**1,680 feet**
Total Elevation Gain:	**1,480 feet**
Parking GPS Coordinates:	**41.17384, -74.16859**
Map:	**NY-NJ TC Southern Harriman-Bear Mountain Trails – Map #118**

Access: Take N.J. Route 17 north to the New York State Thruway and take the first exit, Exit 15A (Sloatsburg). Turn left at the bottom of the ramp onto N.Y. Route 17 north and continue through the village of Sloatsburg. Just beyond the village, turn right at the next traffic light, following the signs for Seven Lakes Drive and Harriman State Park. Proceed ahead on Seven Lakes Drive, crossing an overpass over railroad tracks and an underpass beneath the New York State Thruway, and soon enter Harriman State Park. Proceed for another 0.7 mile to the Reeves Meadow Visitor Center, on the right side of the road, and park in the visitor center parking lot. Note: This parking lot often fills up early on weekends. If the lot is full, additional parking is available on the left side of Seven Lakes Drive, just beyond the entrance to the visitor center.

Description: Walk to the southwestern corner of the parking lot (away from Seven Lakes Drive and on your right, as you face the woods) and find the red-dot-on-white blazes of the Pine Meadow Trail. Turn right, and follow the trail for 0.2 mile as it heads southwest, then turns left into the woods. Where the Pine Meadow Trail turns right, you'll notice three blue-dot-on-white

1

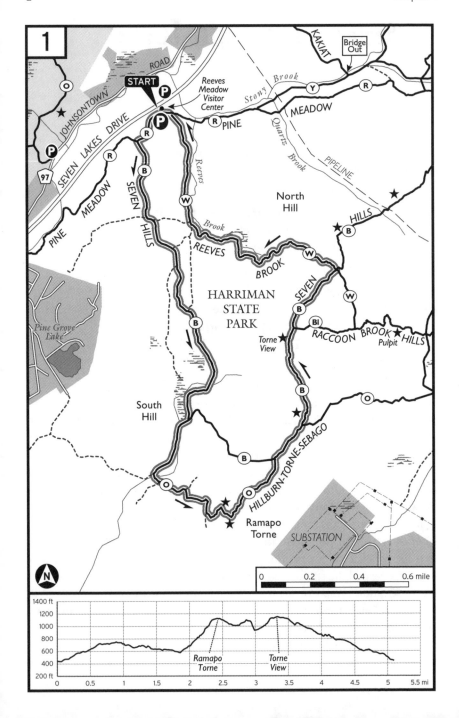

blazes that mark the start of the Seven Hills Trail. Continue ahead, now following the blue-dot-on-white blazes of the Seven Hills Trail, which ascends gradually. After about a third of a mile and a stream crossing, the trail briefly turns left onto a woods road, then turns right, leaving the road, to follow a single-track footpath. For the next mile, the trail continues to gain elevation, occasionally dipping to cross tiny streams. As you pass a small wetland to your right, you can see South Hill in the distance, behind the wetland.

About a mile and a half from the start, the Seven Hills Trail reaches a T-intersection with a woods road. The blue-dot-on-white blazes turn left here, but you should turn right, now following the orange-blazed Hillburn-Torne-Sebago (HTS) Trail. This challenging route up Ramapo Torne was once known as the "Old Red" Trail. It was an informal route until the spring of 2007, when it became an official trail and was marked with orange blazes. The HTS Trail crosses a stream on rocks and then parallels the stream for a third of a mile. At a cairn, turn left, continuing to follow the HTS Trail as it recrosses the stream and continues rather steeply uphill on a woods road.

Along the ridge of the Ramapo Torne

After gaining about 300 vertical feet, the woods road turns right and levels off. A short distance beyond, the trail turns left, leaving the woods road, and scrambles over steep rocks to reach an excellent viewpoint, with southwest-facing views. Continue ahead to an interesting "boulder garden," then bear left and climb a second, slightly less-challenging ledge to even better views over Sterling Forest and Ramapo and Torne Valleys. Proceed around the southern end of the mountain to the top of Ramapo Torne, which offers expansive south and east-facing views of Torne Valley, Hillburn and Mahwah, with the New York State Thruway visible below. This is an excellent spot for a lunch or water break.

Continue to follow the orange blazes of the HTS Trail to the northeast, along the ridge of the Ramapo Torne, for a third of a mile to another junction with the blue-dot-on-white-blazed Seven Hills Trail. Proceed straight ahead along the joint HTS and Seven Hills Trails, which follow the ridge for 0.2 mile. At a high point on the ridge, the two trails split. Bear left here and continue along the blue-dot-on-white blazes of the Seven Hills Trail, which makes a steep descent (this descent can be challenging in icy conditions). The Seven Hills Trail now climbs to Torne View (marked with a cairn) – another great spot for a break. The view from here is a welcome contrast to that from the Ramapo Torne – no highways or buildings are visible. Rather, you see only pristine wilderness – Ramapo Torne to the southwest, and the heavily-forested New York-New Jersey Highlands region to the west.

Heavily-forested view from the Ramapo Torne

Another view from the Ramapo Torne

Soon after Torne View, you'll reach a junction with the black-dot-on-white-blazed Raccoon Brook Hills Trail, which begins on your right. Continue ahead, following the blue-dot-on-white blazes of the Seven Hills Trail, which descends steadily, goes over a slight rise, and finally reaches a hollow (just before a very steep ridge), where it crosses the white-blazed Reeves Brook Trail. You have now covered 3.7 miles and are 1.4 miles from your car.

Turn left onto the white-blazed Reeves Brook Trail, leaving the Seven Hills Trail for good. This winding trail descends gradually, with a few short climbs. In 0.85 mile, after passing a cascade in the brook, the Reeves Brook Trail bears right and joins a woods road. Continue to descend along Reeves Brook for half a mile until the Reeves Brook Trail ends at a T-junction with the red-dot-on-white-blazed Pine Meadow Trail. Turn left onto the Pine Meadow Trail and follow it for 250 feet back to the Reeves Meadow Visitor Center parking lot, where the hike began. 🚶

Chapter 2 **Russian Bear**

Rating:	**Strenuous**
Distance:	**6.2 miles**
Hiking Time:	**4.5 hours**
Attractions:	**Steep terrain, interesting rock formations and panoramic views**
Lowest Elevation:	**440 feet**
Highest Elevation:	**1,220 feet**
Total Elevation Gain:	**1,820 feet**
Parking GPS Coordinates:	**41.17384, -74.16859**
Map:	**NY-NJ TC Southern Harriman-Bear Mountain Trails – Map #118**

Access: Take N.J. Route 17 north to the New York State Thruway and take the first exit, Exit 15A (Sloatsburg). Turn left at the bottom of the ramp onto N.Y. Route 17 north, and continue through the village of Sloatsburg. Just beyond the village, turn right at the next traffic light, following the signs for Seven Lakes Drive and Harriman State Park. Proceed ahead on Seven Lakes Drive, crossing an overpass over railroad tracks and an underpass beneath the New York State Thruway, and soon enter Harriman State Park. Proceed for another 0.7 mile to the Reeves Meadow Visitor Center, on the right side of the road, and park in the visitor center parking lot. Note: This parking lot often fills up early on weekends. If the lot is full, additional parking is available on the left side of Seven Lakes Drive, just beyond the entrance to the visitor center.

Description: From the kiosk on the left side of the parking lot (as you face the woods), head east into the woods, following the red-dot-on-white blazes of the Pine Meadow Trail. In 250 feet, turn right onto the white-blazed Reeves Brook Trail. You'll approach Reeves Brook in 0.2 mile and, in 0.5 mile, pass a

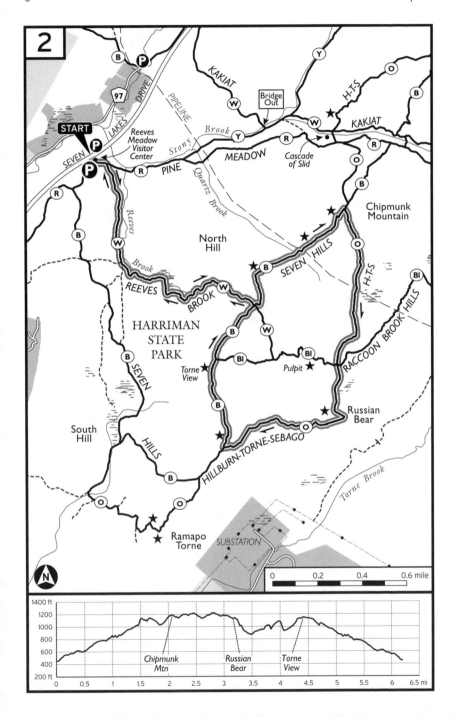

woods road (once known as the Fishline Trail) that leaves to the right. The trail now bears left, and the grade steepens. In another 0.85 mile (1.4 miles from the start of the hike), you'll come to a junction with the blue-dot-on-white-blazed Seven Hills Trail.

Turn left onto the Seven Hills Trail and scramble up the rocks to an excellent viewpoint. This viewpoint (as well as a second viewpoint a short distance beyond) is a great place to stop for a break. The trail now descends for 0.3 mile to cross Quartz Brook on rocks. Just beyond, it crosses the route of a buried gas pipeline and begins to climb Chipmunk Mountain. The views from the crest of the ridge, with its orange-and-white sedimentary rocks, are particularly beautiful. After descending a little, the Seven Hills Trail reaches an intersection with the orange-blazed Hillburn-Torne-Sebago (HTS) Trail. You've now hiked a total of 2.1 miles.

Steep scramble up the Seven Hills Trail

View from the Seven Hills Trail

Along the HTS Trail

Turn sharply right onto the HTS Trail and follow it uphill over the open ridge of Chipmunk Mountain (the trail goes just east of the true summit). In 0.4 mile, the trail recrosses the gas line and, in another 0.4 mile, it crosses the black-on-white-blazed Raccoon Brook Hills (RBH) Trail. In another quarter mile, you'll come out at the top of a cliff (once known as Little Torne). Here, a rock outcrop just to the right of the trail offers excellent views of Torne Valley, the Ramapo Rampart and Ramapo Torne (visible to the right). This spot was renamed "Russian Bear" after a large boulder, said to resemble a performing bear, that was perched at the edge of the cliff (the boulder fell down in 2004). This is a good place for a lunch break.

View from the "Russian Bear"

When you're ready to continue, proceed ahead on the HTS Trail, which descends stone steps into a hollow, crosses a small stream on a wooden bridge, and climbs the next hill on stone steps. The trail now descends rather steeply to another hollow, then climbs to reach a junction with the blue-dot-on-white-blazed Seven Hills Trail. You've hiked a total of 4.0 miles from the start. Turn right onto the Seven Hills Trail, which makes a steep descent (this descent can be challenging in icy conditions). The Seven Hills Trail now climbs to Torne View, which affords a panoramic view over Ramapo Torne to the southwest and the heavily forested New York-New Jersey Highlands region to the west. This is another good spot for a lunch break.

Near the "Russian Bear"

Soon after Torne View, you'll reach a junction with the black-dot-on-white-blazed Raccoon Brook Hills Trail, which begins on your right. Continue ahead, following the blue-dot-on-white blazes of the Seven Hills Trail, which descends steadily, goes over a slight rise, and finally reaches a hollow (just before a very steep ridge), where it crosses the white-blazed Reeves Brook Trail. You have now covered 4.8 miles and are 1.4 miles from your car.

Turn left onto the white-blazed Reeves Brook Trail, now retracing the route you followed earlier on in the hike. This winding trail descends gradually, with a few short climbs. In 0.85 mile, after passing a cascade in the brook, the Reeves Brook Trail bears right and joins a woods road. Continue to descend along Reeves Brook for half a mile until the Reeves Brook Trail ends at a T-junction with the red-dot-on-white-blazed Pine Meadow Trail. Turn left onto the Pine Meadow Trail and follow it for 250 feet back to the Reeves Meadow Visitor Center parking lot, where the hike began. 🥾

Chapter 3   Raccoon Brook Hills

Rating:	**Moderate**
Distance:	**5.7 miles**
Hiking Time:	**3 hours**
Attractions:	**Beautiful cascades, rock caves, rugged terrain and diverse views**
Lowest Elevation:	**440 feet**
Highest Elevation:	**1,160 feet**
Total Elevation Gain:	**1,140 feet**
Parking GPS Coordinates:	**41.17384, -74.16859**
Map:	**NY-NJ TC Southern Harriman-Bear Mountain Trails – Map #118**

Access: Take N.J. Route 17 north to the New York State Thruway and take the first exit, Exit 15A (Sloatsburg). Turn left at the bottom of the ramp onto N.Y. Route 17 north and continue through the village of Sloatsburg. Just beyond the village, turn right at the next traffic light, following the signs for Seven Lakes Drive and Harriman State Park. Proceed ahead on Seven Lakes Drive, crossing an overpass over railroad tracks and an underpass beneath the New York State Thruway, and soon enter Harriman State Park. Proceed for another 0.7 mile to the Reeves Meadow Visitor Center, on the right side of the road, and park in the visitor center parking lot. Note: This parking lot often fills up early on weekends. If the lot is full, additional parking is available on the left side of Seven Lakes Drive, just beyond the entrance to the visitor center.

Description: From the kiosk on the left side of the parking lot (as you face the woods), head east into the woods, following the red-dot-on-white blazes of

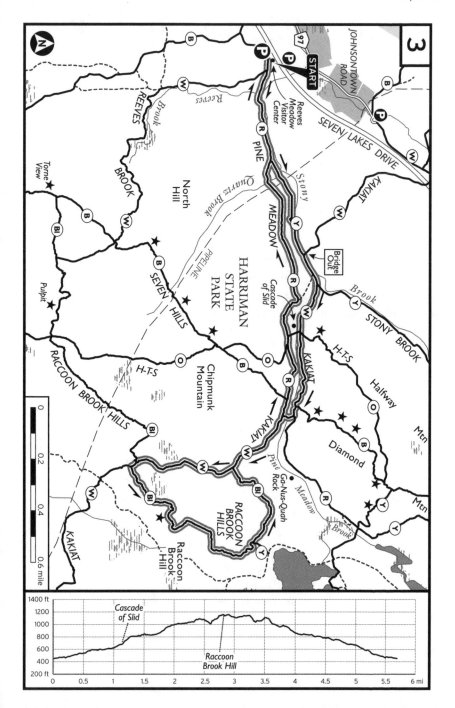

Cascades in Stony Brook

the Pine Meadow Trail. In 250 feet, the white-blazed Reeves Brook Trail begins on the right, but you should continue ahead on the Pine Meadow Trail, which parallels Stony Brook on the left. At 0.4 mile, the Pine Meadow Trail turns right. You should continue straight ahead along Stony Brook, now following the yellow-blazed Stony Brook Trail, which soon goes over a wooden footbridge across Quartz Brook and then crosses the route of a gas pipeline. (Note: During winter months, this section of the Stony Brook Trail often is very icy. Make sure to bring along appropriate traction aids.) In another 0.3 mile, the white-blazed Kakiat Trail joins from the left. Continue ahead along the brook, now following both the Stony Brook and Kakiat Trails. In 750 feet, the joint trails cross a wooden bridge over Pine Meadow Brook and bear right. Just beyond, the Stony Brook Trail turns left, but you should continue ahead, now following the white blazes of the Kakiat Trail.

The Kakiat Trail climbs between boulders alongside the cascading Pine Meadow Brook, which is on your right. The roaring water becomes louder and more dramatic as you reach the Cascade of Slid at 1.2 miles. Here, the orange-blazed Hillburn-Torne-Sebago Trail joins from the left and almost immediately leaves to the right, crossing Pine Meadow Brook on a wooden footbridge.

You should continue straight ahead, continuing to follow the white-blazed Kakiat Trail. After passing a natural rock shelter on the left, the blue-on-white-blazed Seven Hills Trail joins from the left. Just beyond, turn right and cross Pine Meadow Brook on another wooden footbridge, following the co-aligned Kakiat (white), Pine Meadow (red square on white) and Seven Hills (blue dot on white) Trails.

On the other side of the bridge, turn left and continue to follow the white-blazed Kakiat Trail, which climbs gradually for about a third of a mile through mountain laurel thickets until it reaches the start of the black-on-white-blazed Raccoon Brook Hills Trail (RBH) on your left, with an interesting rock formation on the right. You'll be following the RBH Trail in a short while, but for now, continue ahead on the white-blazed Kakiat Trail, which levels off and soon turns left to cross an intermittent stream. It continues through a dense mountain laurel thicket and climbs through an opening in the rocks to the top of a second rock formation, where the black-on-white-blazed RBH Trail joins from the right. In 125 feet, the two trails diverge. The Kakiat Trail continues straight ahead, but you should turn left onto the black-on-white-blazed RBH Trail. You have now traveled 2.4 miles.

Along the Raccoon Brook Hills Trail

After a gentle descent, you'll begin a moderately steep, two-stage climb of Raccoon Brook Hill's southern summit, soon reaching an open rock ledge, with stunted pitch pines and scenic views. Just ahead, the ascent becomes very steep, with a wooden ladder placed near the top to assist you as you climb. At the top (elevation 1,150 feet), the trail comes out on a rock ledge that offers a panoramic southwest-facing view over Torne Valley, with the Ramapo Mountains of New Jersey beyond. The trail now heads northeast, passing partial views of the New York City skyline to your right. It then descends through thick mountain laurel, comes out in an open area, and climbs slightly to reach the northern summit of Raccoon Brook Hill, with seasonal views of Pine Meadow Lake to the northeast.

Ladder on the Raccoon Brook Hills Trail

The RBH Trail now turns left and makes a short, steep descent into a hollow, passing the trailhead of the yellow-on-white-blazed Poached Egg Trail on your right at 3.35 miles. Bear left at this intersection to continue on the RBH Trail, which climbs another hill and reaches a seasonal view of the Almost Perpendicular rock formation (see Chapter 8) straight ahead in the distance (to the northwest). The trail now makes two more short, steep descents. At the base of the second descent, look for a tiny passageway through the rocks behind you on the right. Indian artifacts were found inside caves in these rocks (the artifacts are currently housed in the Trailside Museum at Bear Mountain). In another 250 feet, the RBH Trail crosses Raccoon Brook and ends at a junction with the white-blazed Kakiat Trail. This junction, at 3.8 miles, should look familiar to you, since you passed it earlier.

Southwest-facing view from Raccoon Brook Hill

Turn right onto the Kakiat Trail and follow it downhill for a third of a mile. When the white blazes turn right to cross a wooden bridge, you should continue straight ahead (do not cross the bridge), now following the red-square-on-white-blazed Pine Meadow Trail, which is wide and easy to follow. You'll encounter a number of intersecting trails along the way, but just be sure to follow the red-square-on-white blazes for 1.55 miles all the way back to your car. ⓕ

Chapter 4   Lake Sebago, Stony Brook and Diamond Mountain

Shorter Hike   *Rating:*   **Moderate**
Distance: **5.1 miles**
Hiking Time: **2.5 hours**
Attractions: **Beautiful lake and cascading brook**
Lowest Elevation: **530 feet**
Highest Elevation: **955 feet**
Total Elevation Gain: **770 feet**

Longer Hike   *Rating:*   **Moderate to strenuous**
Distance: **6.4 miles**
Hiking Time: **4 hours**
Attractions: **Beautiful lake, cascading brook, panoramic views from Diamond Mountain, and Cascade of Slid**
Lowest Elevation: **530 feet**
Highest Elevation: **1,242 feet**
Total Elevation Gain: **1,310 feet**

Longest Hike   *Rating:*   **Strenuous**
Distance: **7.8 miles**
Hiking Time: **5 hours**
Attractions: **Beautiful lake, cascading brook, panoramic views from Diamond and Halfway Mountains, and Cascade of Slid**
Lowest Elevation: **530 feet**
Highest Elevation: **1,242 feet**
Total Elevation Gain: **1,725 feet**

Parking GPS Coordinates: **41.18015, -74.16351**
Map: **NY-NJ TC Southern Harriman-Bear Mountain Trails – Map #118**

Access: Take N.J. Route 17 north to the New York State Thruway and take the first exit, Exit 15A (Sloatsburg). Turn left at the bottom of the ramp onto N.Y. Route 17 north, and continue through the village of Sloatsburg. Just beyond the village,

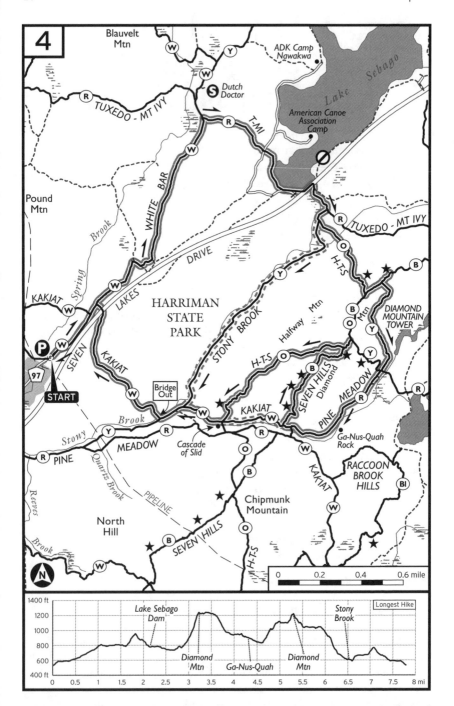

turn right at the next traffic light, following the signs for Seven Lakes Drive and Harriman State Park. Cross an overpass over railroad tracks and continue along Seven Lakes Drive for 0.7 mile, passing under the New York State Thruway. Just before reaching a large sign "Welcome to Harriman State Park," turn left at a sign for Johnsontown Road, immediately reaching a stop sign at a T-intersection. Turn right, proceed for 1.2 miles to the end of the road, and park along the right side of the circle.

Note: **All of the hikes described in this chapter require you to cross, near the end of the hike, the footbridge of the Kakiat Trail over Stony Brook. This bridge was washed away by Hurricane Irene in August 2011, and as of the date of the publication of this book (March 2015), it has not yet been replaced. Crossing the brook at this location without a bridge is dangerous and not advised. Until the bridge is replaced, it is recommended that you choose an alternative hike.**

Description: Three possible loop hikes are described in this chapter – the farther you are willing to go, the more highlights you will see.

Begin by walking to the northeastern end of the cul-de-sac, exactly halfway around the circle. Here you will find the start of the White Bar Trail, marked by three horizontal white blazes. Follow the blazes gently uphill, heading northeast on a grassy woods road (Old Johnsontown Road). In 0.3 mile, the Kakiat Trail, marked by vertical white blazes, joins from the left, briefly runs concurrently with the White Bar Trail, then leaves to the right. The Kakiat Trail will be your return route, but for now, continue ahead on the White Bar Trail.

In another 0.15 mile, the White Bar Trail turns left, passes several huge boulders, then turns right at a fork. A short distance beyond, the trail turns left, passes between two green metal gateposts, and heads uphill. After reaching the crest of the rise, the trail begins to descend. At the base of the descent, you will notice a marsh on the left. Soon, you'll see (between the trail and the marsh) a cellar hole, which marks the site of the 19th century homestead site of John Frederick Helms, known as the "Old Dutch Doctor." Helms grew medicinal herbs, such as ginseng, here.

Just beyond, the Tuxedo-Mt. Ivy Trail (T-MI), marked by red-dash-on-white blazes, joins from the right. Turn right here, leaving the White Bar Trail, and follow the T-MI Trail uphill through a rocky area. After climbing over a hill, the trail begins to descend, crossing a paved camp road on the way down. In another 250 feet, the trail turns right and passes through a mountain laurel thicket, paralleling the shore of beautiful Lake Sebago. After briefly coming out at the lakeshore (with panoramic views over the lake), the trail reaches Seven Lakes Drive. It crosses the road, turns left, and follows the sidewalk across the Lake Sebago dam. At the other side of the dam, it turns right, goes under the guardrail, and heads down along the eastern side of the spillway. You've now gone 2.2 miles from the start of the hike.

Lake Sebago from Diamond Mountain

At the base of the dam, the unmarked Woodtown Road goes off to the left, but you should continue ahead, following the T-MI Trail, which soon bears left to parallel Stony Brook. In a quarter mile from the Lake Sebago dam, the T-MI Trail crosses a tributary stream. Just beyond the stream crossing, the orange-blazed Hillburn-Torne-Sebago Trail (HTS) begins on the right. The T-MI turns left here and heads uphill, but you should continue straight, now following the orange blazes of the HTS Trail. Continue along the HTS Trail for 400 feet to a junction with the yellow-blazed Stony Brook Trail. If you wish to do the "short" 5.1-mile hike, follow the directions below, in the section entitled "Shorter Hike." For a 6.4- or 7.8-mile hike, skip ahead to the section entitled "Longer Hikes."

Shorter Hike: The orange-blazed HTS Trail bears left here, but you should continue straight ahead, following the yellow-blazed Stony Brook Trail. This relatively level trail bears left to cross Diamond Creek, then parallels the cascading Stony Brook for over a mile. About 3.8 miles from the start of the hike, the white-blazed Kakiat Trail joins from the left. Turn right here, now following both white and yellow blazes, and cross a footbridge over Pine Meadow Brook. To complete your hike, skip ahead now to the section entitled "Return Trip."

Longer Hikes: Bear left, continuing to follow the orange-blazed HTS Trail uphill. After making a two-part crossing of Diamond Creek, the climb steepens. As you climb and scramble up Diamond Mountain, there are several limited views of Lake Sebago. At the top, the HTS Trail reaches a junction with the blue-dot-on-white-blazed Seven Hills Trail. Turn left here, leaving the HTS Trail and following the blue-dot-on-white blazes in a northeasterly direction. You've now gone about three miles from the start of the hike.

In 0.1 mile, you'll pass the end of the yellow-blazed Diamond Mountain-Tower Trail on your right, and in another 0.1 mile, you'll reach an unobstructed view of Lake Sebago on your left. On a clear day, you can see all the way to the northeastern Catskill Mountains (visible directly behind the northern arm of the lake). This is a good place for a lunch or water break.

Now retrace your steps for 0.1 mile, returning to the junction with the Diamond Mountain-Tower Trail (marked by a triple-yellow blaze on your left). Turn left and follow the yellow blazes, which climb gently over orange-colored bedrock to the site of the former fire tower. The trail now bears right (the old fire tower road heads downhill to the left), passing limited views of Lake Wanoksink

DAN BALOGH

Steep climb of Diamond Mountain on the Seven Hills Trail

North-facing view from the Seven Hills Trail climbing Diamond Mountain

and Pine Meadow Lake as it descends. Near the base of the descent, the trail passes to the right of an incomplete dam, which was intended to form Lake Oonotookwa ("place of cattails"). If you wish to explore the area, be careful on the loose rocks leading to the dam.

After passing a concrete tank (built in 1934 as a septic tank for the proposed camps along Pine Meadow Lake; the camps were never constructed, and the tank was never used), the Diamond Mountain-Tower Trail reaches a junction with the red-dot-on-white-blazed Pine Meadow Trail. The Diamond Mountain-Tower Trail turns right here, but you should continue straight ahead (not left), now following the Pine Meadow Trail.

Continue ahead past an old foundation (the former headquarters of three Civilian Conservation Corps camps), and in 0.4 mile, you'll reach two huge boulders known as Ga-Nus-Quah (Stone Giants). Here, you'll find an interesting passageway through the rock and the beautiful, cascading Pine Meadow Brook. You've now gone about 4.3 miles from the start, and this is a good spot for a break. In another quarter mile, the Pine Meadow Trail reaches a footbridge (on the left) and meets up with the Seven Hills and Kakiat Trails. The Pine Meadow Trail turns left to cross the bridge, but you should continue straight ahead on the co-aligned Seven Hills (blue-dot-on-white) and Kakiat (white) Trails. In about 200 feet, the trails split. Here you need to decide whether you will be taking the steep and challenging 7.8-mile hike or the more moderate 6.4-mile hike.

For the 7.8-mile hike, skip ahead to the section entitled "Longest Hike." For the 6.4-mile hike, continue straight ahead on the white-blazed Kakiat Trail. You'll pass a bridge on your left and be joined briefly by the orange-blazed HTS Trail at 4.85 miles. Continuing on the Kakiat Trail, you'll go by a scenic cascade known as the "Cascade of Slid" and pass between huge boulders as you descend gradually along the brook. At 5.1 miles, you'll reach a junction with the yellow-blazed Stony Brook Trail. Continue ahead, now following both white and yellow blazes, then bear left to cross a footbridge over Pine Meadow Brook. To complete your hike, skip ahead to the section entitled "Return Trip."

Longest Hike: Note: You should not attempt this part of the hike if conditions are wet or snowy or if you are afraid of heights! Turn right, following the blue-dot-on-white blazed Seven Hills Trail, which soon bears right again, climbing up a very steep rock ledge. The trail switches back to the left and continues climbing steeply along the edge of a cliff. Note the beautiful pitch pines along the upper part of the cliff. There are several panoramic views to the north and northwest as you make your ascent.

Just short of the summit, at 5.25 miles, the Seven Hills Trail reaches a junction with the orange-blazed HTS Trail. Continue ahead on the joint Seven Hills-HTS Trails for about 250 feet to the 1,242-foot summit of Diamond Mountain, with

DAN BALOGH

Pine Meadow Lake from Diamond Mountain

Cascade of Slid

360-degree views, then retrace your steps to the junction and bear right to continue along the HTS Trail. The trail descends steeply for a short distance but soon levels off, following the ridge of Halfway Mountain to a mostly unobstructed, west-facing viewpoint. From the viewpoint, the HTS Trail descends gradually, returning you to Pine Meadow Brook and the Kakiat Trail at 6.15 miles.

At the brook, the HTS Trail bears left toward a footbridge, but you should turn right (do not cross the bridge), now following the white-blazed Kakiat Trail. You will go by a scenic cascade known as the "Cascade of Slid" and pass between huge boulders as you descend gradually along the brook. At 6.4 miles, you'll reach a junction with the yellow-blazed Stony Brook Trail. Continue ahead, now following both white and yellow blazes, then bear left to cross a footbridge over Pine Meadow Brook.

Return Trip: About 750 feet after crossing the footbridge over Pine Meadow Brook, the white-blazed Kakiat Trail splits off to the right. Turn right, leaving the Stony Brook Trail, and follow the Kakiat Trail, which crosses a second footbridge – this one, over Stony Brook – and climbs through an evergreen forest. (Note: As of February 2015, the footbridge over Stony Brook was out, and it is dangerous and inadvisable to cross the brook in the absence of the bridge.) After a level section (an old farmsite), the trail climbs to the crest of a hill, then descends on a woods road to Seven Lakes Drive. It crosses the road and heads downhill, reaching the Old Johnsontown Road in 150 feet. Turn left on this road, joining the horizontal-white-blazed White Bar Trail.

The Kakiat Trail soon turns off to the right, but you should continue straight on the grassy woods road, following the White Bar Trail for 0.3 mile back to your car at the Johnsontown Road Circle. ⚲

Chapter 5 Pine Meadow Lake and the Ramapo Escarpment

Shorter Hike

Rating:	**Moderate to strenuous**
Distance:	**6.0 miles**
Hiking Time:	**4 hours**
Total Elevation Gain:	**1,430 feet**

Longer Hike

Rating:	**Strenuous**
Distance:	**7.9 miles**
Hiking Time:	**5.5 hours**
Total Elevation Gain:	**1,620 feet**

Attractions:	**Less-crowded hiking route to a popular, scenic lake. Interesting rock formations, a stone shelter and good views from Harriman's eastern escarpment**
Lowest Elevation:	**400 feet**
Highest Elevation:	**1,200 feet**
Parking GPS Coordinates:	**41.17452, -74.08487**
Map:	**NY-NJ TC Southern Harriman-Bear Mountain Trails – Map #118**

Access: Take N.J. Route 17 north to the New York State Thruway and take the first exit, Exit 15A (Sloatsburg). Turn right at the bottom of the ramp onto Route 59 east and follow it for 1.6 miles to the first traffic light in the village of Suffern. Turn left at the light onto U.S. Route 202 north, follow it for 5.4 miles, then turn left into the Town of Ramapo Equestrian Center. Continue over a small bridge and park on the left, just before the white, fenced-in riding area.

Description: Two possible loop hikes are described in this chapter. Both hikes take you up to scenic Pine Meadow Lake, but the longer hike leads you around the lake. The longer hike is slightly more difficult to navigate as it follows unmarked trails for part of the way.

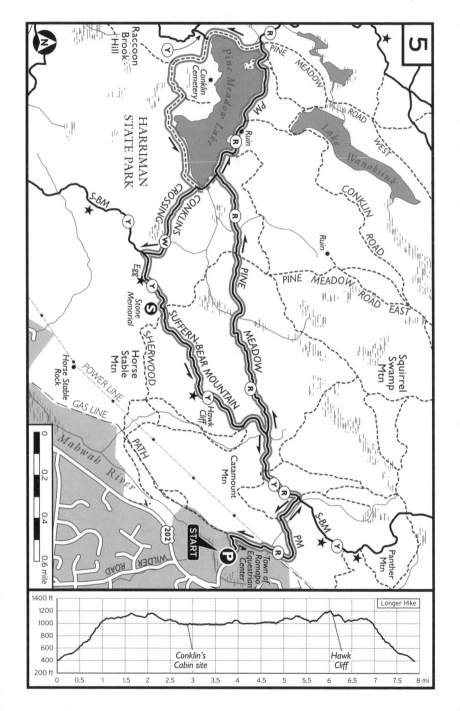

Pine Meadow Lake

Begin by circling counter-clockwise around the right side of the white fence until you reach the start of the red-square-on-white-blazed Pine Meadow Trail on your right. You will be following this trail for the next 2.75 miles (if you do the shorter hike) or 3.5 miles (if you do the longer hike).

Follow the blazes uphill for 0.1 mile and then turn right onto a gas line service road. In about 750 feet, rock cairns and blazes lead you to the left under the power lines, then right on a parallel service road, crossing Guyascutus Brook. Soon the trail leaves the power line service road and turns left on a woods road, beginning a moderately steep climb. It recrosses the brook, turns right and climbs alongside it.

At 0.85 mile, after a rather steep climb along the brook, the Pine Meadow Trail reaches a junction with the yellow-blazed Suffern-Bear Mountain (S-BM) Trail. Here, the woods road you have been following along the brook continues straight ahead, but you should turn left, following the co-aligned red-square-on-white and yellow trails up Catamount Mountain. In 0.45 mile, after leveling off and crossing a small stream, the trails diverge. The yellow-blazed S-BM Trail bears left, but you should bear right, following the red-square-on-white-blazed Pine Meadow Trail.

For the next mile, you will pass through hardwood forests, marshy spots and mountain laurel thickets, eventually crossing unpaved Pine Meadow Road East (identified only by a rusted "Foot Travel Only" sign). In another 0.4 mile,

Stone ruins of pumphouse

you'll reach beautiful Pine Meadow Lake and a junction with the white-blazed Conklins Crossing Trail. You have now traveled 2.75 miles and must decide whether to take the shorter or the longer hike.

Shorter hike: Turn left onto the white-blazed Conklins Crossing Trail. Follow the white blazes for 0.6 mile, crossing two streams and an unmarked trail, and then heading uphill. The white trail terminates at a junction with the yellow-blazed S-BM Trail, marked by large boulders. Turn left onto the S-BM Trail. You have now hiked a total of 3.35 miles. To complete your hike, skip ahead to the section entitled "Return Trip."

Longer hike: Continue straight ahead on the red-on-white-blazed Pine Meadow Trail, which follows the northeast shore of Pine Meadow Lake. You will notice some old, rusted pipes along the trail. These were installed by workers of the Civilian Conservation Corps (CCC) in the 1930s to serve children's camps that were to be built along the lake. The camps were never built, and the pipes were never used.

In about 500 feet, you'll reach the site of Conklin's Cabin, which was inhabited by the Conklin family between 1779 and 1935. Nothing remains of the cabin, but a rock ledge on the left offers a panoramic view of the lake. Then, in another 0.2 mile, you'll see a stone building on the left. This building was intended to be used as a pumphouse for the water system around the lake.

Continue along the Pine Meadow Trail, keeping the lake on your left. Near the northern end of the lake (3.5 miles into the hike), an unmarked trail leads a short distance to the left, out to a scenic point on the lake. This is an excellent and very popular spot for a lunch break.

Return to the Pine Meadow Trail and turn left, continuing north along the lake (with the lakeshore still on your left). When you reach an unmarked dirt road (Pine Meadow Road West), turn left, leaving the Pine Meadow Trail, and follow the road, which crosses a bridge and heads slightly away from the water. After passing a junction with a yellow-on-white trail (the Poached Egg Trail), which leaves to the right, the road climbs and then descends to a junction with another woods road. Continue straight ahead, and in about 0.2 mile, you will pass an old cement foundation on your right. Pay close attention as, in less than 0.1 mile, you will need to turn right onto a unmarked path which runs along the top of a stone wall.

The stone wall was built by the CCC to support the now-rusty pipes that were intended to supply water to camps along the lake. The narrow footpath is clear and easy to follow, but the footing can be rather rough in places, and caution should be exercised. At one point, the footpath turns sharply left and begins to run parallel to the shore of Pine Meadow Lake, but some distance from the water. Follow the narrow path until it ends at a junction with the white-blazed Conklins Crossing Trail.

Stone Memorial Shelter

Hikers at Hawk Cliff

Turn right, following the white blazes for 0.5 mile uphill. The white trail terminates at a junction with the yellow-blazed S-BM Trail, marked by several large boulders. Turn left onto the S-BM Trail. You have now hiked a total of 5.2 miles.

Return trip: You will be following the yellow-blazed S-BM Trail for the next 1.85 miles. The S-BM Trail is a 23-mile footpath that follows the eastern escarpment of the Ramapo Mountains, providing occasional views of the lower Hudson Valley and the New York City skyline. In 0.15 mile, you'll reach "The Egg" – a huge boulder on your right, with a panoramic view to the southeast from the top.

From "The Egg," you'll descend, cross a small stream, and climb to reach the Stone Memorial Shelter – a sturdy shelter built in 1935. Swing around the front of the shelter (blazes may be hard to follow here), then bear left and follow the yellow blazes across a woods road. The trail now climbs steadily and, after a few minor ups-and-downs, emerges on the edge of the ridge at Hawk Cliff, with panoramic views. In another half mile, you'll be joined on the left by the familiar red-square-on-white blazes of the Pine Meadow Trail. Follow the co-aligned red-square-on-white and yellow trails for the next 0.45 mile, and when the trails diverge, turn right, following the red-square-on-white blazes.

If the trail looks familiar, it is because you followed this exact route at the start of your hike. Follow the Pine Meadow Trail downhill, crossing under the power line, and briefly follow along the gas line. Be alert for a sharp left turn, and follow the red-square-on-white blazes as they descend to the equestrian center and back to your car. 🚶

Chapter 6 Jackie Jones Mountain and Big Hill

Single Loop

Rating:	**Moderate**
Distance:	**4.3 miles**
Hiking Time:	**3 hours**
Total Elevation Gain:	**1,020 feet**
Attractions:	**Ruins of ORAK, panoramic views from fire tower and Big Hill Shelter**

Double Loop

Rating:	**Moderate to strenuous**
Distance:	**6.5 miles**
Hiking Time:	**4 hours**
Total Elevation Gain:	**1,300 feet**
Attractions:	**Ruins of ORAK, panoramic views from fire tower and Big Hill Shelter, scenic reservoir**

Lowest Elevation:	**890 feet**
Highest Elevation:	**1,276 feet**
Parking GPS Coordinates:	**41.22978, -74.06042**
Map:	**NY-NJ TC Southern Harriman-Bear Mountain Trails – Map #118**

Access: Take the Palisades Interstate Parkway north to Exit 14 and turn left onto Willow Grove Road (County Route 98). In about two miles, the road joins County Route 106, which comes in from the right. Continue for another 0.2 mile, and park in a parking area on the left, just before crossing a bridge over a stream.

Alternatively, you can take N.J. Route 17 north to the New York State Thruway and take the first exit, Exit 15A (Sloatsburg). Turn left at the bottom of the ramp onto N.Y. Route 17 north and continue through the village of Sloatsburg. Just beyond the village, turn right at the next traffic light, following the signs for Seven Lakes Drive and Harriman State Park. Continue to follow Seven Lakes Drive for 7.1 miles to the Kanawauke Circle. At the circle, turn right onto Route 106 (Kanawauke Road) and follow it for 3.2 miles to a parking area on the right, just beyond a bridge over a stream.

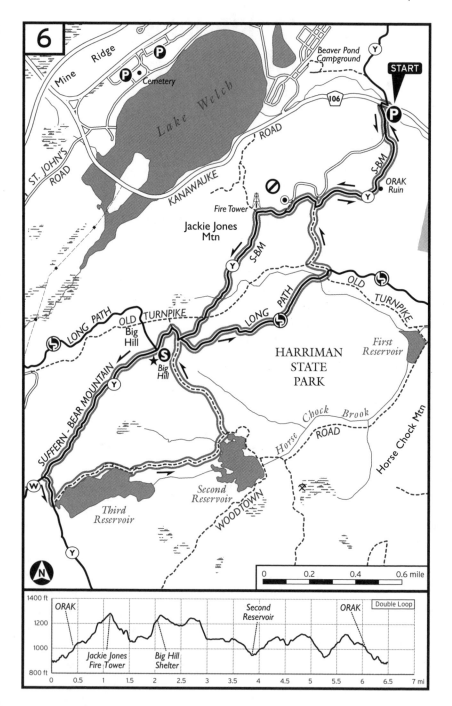

Description: This hike is filled with relics and remnants of the past. Old roads and ruins of stone buildings remind the visitor that this area was not always the forest preserve it is today. The shorter version of this hike features mountaintop views, a fire tower, vernal ponds and an interesting mansion ruin. The longer version adds two scenic lakes and a bit more mountaintop trekking to the journey – as well as the chance to see chunks of slag along the shore of Third Reservoir, which serve as evidence of past mining activity nearby. Either version is a good choice for a group hike because you are never more than 1.25 miles from the safety of your car or the Big Hill Shelter.

Single Loop: From the parking area, walk west along Route 106 for 300 feet, crossing over Minisceongo Creek. Turn left at the gated paved road and proceed uphill, following the yellow blazes of the Suffern-Bear Mountain (S-BM) Trail. You will be following the S-BM Trail for the next two miles – all the way to the Big Hill Shelter.

In a quarter of a mile, the S-BM Trail bears left onto a woods road and soon reaches the stone ruins of a large estate. Known as ORAK, the mansion was built in 1923 by George Briggs Buchanan, a vice president of the Corn Products Refining Company, which manufactured Karo syrup (Orak is Karo spelled backwards). After Buchanan died in 1939, his heirs sold the mansion to the park, and it was demolished in 1973. You will pass this way again near the end of your hike, so you either can explore the grounds now or wait until later.

Resting at the ruins of ORAK

Soon, you'll reach a fork in the trail. The unmarked woods road that comes in from the left will be your return route, but for now, bear right to continue on the S-BM Trail. The trail soon bears left, leaving the woods road, and climbs to a limited southeast-facing viewpoint. A short distance beyond, it passes communications

Jackie Jones Fire Tower

towers to the right and soon arrives at the 1,276-foot summit of Jackie Jones Mountain, marked by a steel fire tower. Built in 1928, the 60-foot-high tower offers a panoramic view over Lake Welch to the north and the Hudson River to the southeast. You've now gone 1.1 miles from the start of the hike.

View from the Jackie Jones Fire Tower

The S-BM Trail now descends, steeply in places. After crossing a stream, it climbs a little and then resumes its steep descent. At the base of the descent, it crosses another stream and then the Old Turnpike – a wide woods road, which is now the route of a gas pipeline. After ascending slightly, it reaches a junction with the aqua-blazed Long Path, which comes in from the left.

Continue ahead on the joint S-BM/Long Path, which turns right onto a woods road. A short distance ahead, the joint trails turn left and climb to the Big Hill Shelter. Built in 1927, this stone shelter offers a panoramic view to the south, with the New York City skyline visible in the distance on a clear day. It also provides refuge from sun, wind, rain or snow. You've hiked for just over two miles, and this is a good spot to take a break.

Big Hill Shelter

When you're ready to continue, go back and descend on the S-BM/Long Path, following the same route you took up to the shelter. When you reach the fork where the two trails diverge, bear right and continue on the Long Path. The Long Path climbs a little and then begins a steady descent, passing a vernal pond along the way. After crossing a stream, you'll reach the wide Old Turnpike, with posts marking its use as a gas pipeline. You've hiked for about 0.9 mile on the Long Path from the point where it diverged from the S-BM Trail.

Leave the Long Path route here and turn left onto the Old Turnpike, which heads uphill for about 500 feet. At the crest of the rise – just before reaching a post with the number 712 – turn right onto an unmarked woods road, which heads north, uphill. In about 0.3 mile, you'll reach a junction with the yellow-blazed S-BM Trail. The yellow blazes head both right and straight ahead, but you should turn right, now retracing your steps along the S-BM Trail. Follow the trail downhill past the ruins of ORAK and back to Route 106 (Kanawauke Road), then turn right on Route 106 to reach the parking area where the hike began.

Double Loop: Follow the single-loop hike description to the Big Hill Shelter. From there, do not double back but instead, continue on following the yellow blazes of the S-BM Trail along the top of Big Hill for another 0.85 mile. Along the way, you hike over bare rock and finally descend to reach the eastern terminus of the white-blazed Breakneck Mountain Trail on your right. Continue following the yellow S-BM Trail for another 750 feet down to the Third Reservoir.

As soon as you reach the reservoir, turn left and follow an unmarked path along the northern shore of the reservoir, with the water on your right. In 0.4 mile, turn left at the "No Trespassing" sign and continue for another 500 feet to a fork in the road, where you will bear left. Continue on this road for another 0.3 mile, through a hardwood forest, to the Second Reservoir. Turn left here, keeping the water on your right, and watch closely for a left-hand turn which comes up in 500 feet. This woods road should be marked by a rock cairn.

After turning left, you'll proceed generally uphill for another 0.5 mile until you meet up with the yellow S-BM Trail and aqua Long Path. At this junction, bear right, then immediately turn right again to continue on the Long Path. The Long Path climbs a little and then begins a steady descent, passing a vernal pond along the way. After crossing a stream, you'll reach the wide Old Turnpike, with posts marking its use as a gas pipeline.

Leave the Long Path route here and turn left onto the Old Turnpike, which heads uphill for about 500 feet. At the crest of the rise – just before reaching a post with the number 712 – turn right onto an unmarked woods road, which heads north, uphill. In about 0.3 mile, you'll reach a junction with the yellow-blazed S-BM Trail. The yellow blazes head both right and straight ahead, but you should turn right, now retracing your steps along the S-BM Trail. Follow the trail downhill past the ruins of ORAK and back to Route 106 (Kanawauke Road), then turn right on Route 106 to reach the parking area where the hike began. 🏃

Chapter 7 Sleater Hill and Almost Perpendicular

Shorter Hike

Rating:	**Easy to moderate**
Distance:	**4.6 miles**
Hiking Time:	**3 hours**
Attractions:	**Scenic vistas, wetlands and wildlife viewing opportunities in Dater Mountain Nature County Park**
Lowest Elevation:	**520 feet**
Highest Elevation:	**715 feet**
Total Elevation Gain:	**835 feet**

Longer Hike

Rating:	**Moderate to strenuous**
Distance:	**5.2 miles**
Hiking Time:	**3.5 hours**
Attractions:	**Panoramic vistas of Harriman State Park from Almost Perpendicular, wetlands and wildlife viewing opportunities in Dater Mountain Nature County Park**
Lowest Elevation:	**520 feet**
Highest Elevation:	**940 feet**
Total Elevation Gain:	**1,140 feet**
Parking GPS Coordinates:	**41.18015, -74.16351**
Map:	**NY-NJ TC Southern Harriman-Bear Mountain Trails – Map #118**

Access: Take N.J. Route 17 north to the New York State Thruway and take the first exit, Exit 15A (Sloatsburg). Turn left at the bottom of the ramp onto N.Y. Route 17 north, and continue through the village of Sloatsburg. Just beyond the village, turn right at the next traffic light, following the signs for Seven Lakes Drive and Harriman State Park. Cross an overpass over railroad tracks and continue along

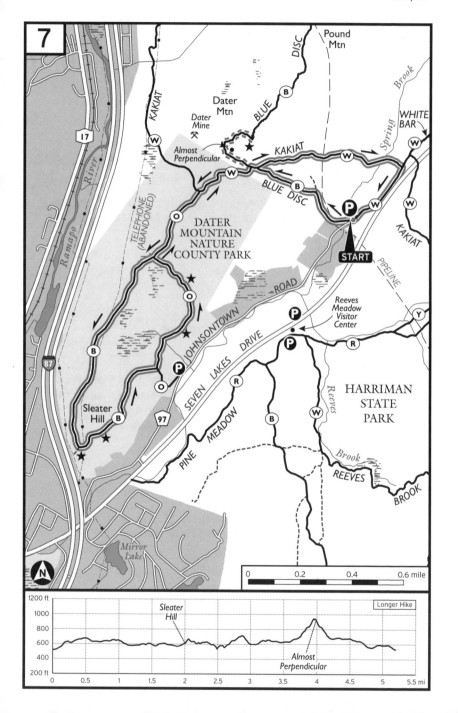

Seven Lakes Drive for 0.7 mile, passing under the New York State Thruway. Just before reaching a large sign "Welcome to Harriman State Park," turn left at a sign for Johnsontown Road, immediately reaching a T-intersection. Turn right, proceed for 1.2 miles to the end of the road, and park along the right side of the circle.

Description: The expansion of Rockland County's Dater Mountain Nature County Park to 351 acres in August 2005 preserved the habitat of two endangered species, the Northern Cricket Frog and Allegheny Wood Rat. For hikers, it opened up new opportunities for exploration in and around the southwestern corner of Harriman State Park.

Begin your hike by walking southwest on Johnsontown Road, away from the circle. Almost immediately, just past a sign for Rockland County Route 97, a triple blue-on-white blaze on a tree to the right marks the start of the Blue Disc Trail. Turn right onto this trail, which proceeds uphill on a paved road. The trail crosses the route of the Columbia Gas Transmission pipeline, then follows a footpath through the woods parallel to the pipeline. At 0.2 mile, it turns left onto a woods road and soon resumes a gentle climb, passing through a young forest of witch hazel, sassafras, maple and mixed hardwoods, with giant boulders along the way.

View of Sloatsburg and the New York State Thruway from Sleater Hill

At 0.5 mile, bear right at a fork in the woods road. Just beyond, the white blazes of the Kakiat Trail join from the right. In 125 feet, when the trails diverge, turn left and continue on the white-blazed Kakiat Trail. After passing a huge boulder on the left of the trail, the woods road curves sharply to the left. Here, a less distinct woods road on the right leads up to the Dater Mine.

A short distance beyond, as the Kakiat Trail curves to the right, you'll notice a cairn, with an exposed bedrock ledge straight ahead. Here, a triple orange blaze marks the start of the Orange Trail. Continue ahead, leaving the Kakiat Trail, and follow the Orange Trail, which heads southwest on a woods road, passing numerous rock outcrops and several vernal ponds. This is an excellent place to look for such wildlife as songbirds, spring peepers and wild turkeys.

After 0.35 mile on the Orange Trail, you'll reach a junction. Here, the orange blazes bear left, but you should continue ahead on the woods road, now following the Blue Trail. Together, the Orange and Blue Trails form a short but scenic ridgeline loop.

Just beyond, you'll cross a stream – the outlet of a wetland on the left. You'll pass several wetlands on the left along this section of the trail. During warmer weather, the sounds of birds and amphibians in these wetlands provide a nice distraction from the sounds of the New York State Thruway, below to the right, which grow louder as you approach Sleater Hill. Keep an eye out to your right for seasonal views of Tuxedo and Sloatsburg. Along the way, you may find coyote scat, especially where you pass several unmarked side roads to the right.

About 0.8 mile from the start of the Blue Trail, the woods road followed by the trail curves sharply to the left. Here, a side road goes off to the right. A quick side trip on this road leads to a glacial erratic, a power line and a good westward view of Sloatsburg and the Thruway below.

After taking in the view, return to the trail and turn right. Just beyond, the Blue Trail leaves the woods road and continues on a footpath. It climbs Sleater Hill, passing just to the right of the summit at 2.0 miles. It then descends, soon reaching a rock outcrop on the right. From here, you can see the Mirror Lake area of Sloatsburg as well as Nordkop Mountain and South Hill, with the Ramapo Torne visible behind South Hill. The Blue Trail descends further through a hardwood forest. After crossing a woods road, it levels off, then resumes a gradual descent, ending at 2.55 miles at an intersection with the Orange Trail.

Turn left onto the Orange Trail, which heads uphill and then descends to cross a small stream in a narrow hollow, with a rock ledge looming above. After climbing some more, you'll reach a viewpoint over Halfway Mountain, North

View of Halfway Mountain, North Hill and South Hill from the Orange Trail

Hill and South Hill, with the Reeves Meadow Visitor Center visible on your right when there are no leaves on the trees. This is a nice spot for lunch or a short break. Then, at 3.0 miles, at the height of the land, there is a view of Dater Mountain and the ledges of Almost Perpendicular from open rocks about 50 feet to the right of the trail.

The Orange Trail now descends to reach an intersection with the Blue Trail, completing the ridgeline loop. Continue to follow the Orange Trail as it turns right onto a woods road and returns to its eastern terminus at 3.5 miles. You should recognize this spot by the bedrock slab and cairn you passed earlier in the hike. Here, you should bear right and head east along the white-blazed Kakiat Trail. At 3.7 miles, you'll bear left at a fork and reach a junction with the Blue Disc Trail. From here, you will continue along the white-blazed Kakiat Trail to return to your car, but if you wish, you can take an 0.6-mile, out-and-back side trip to a spectacular view from Almost Perpendicular.

Side Trip: If you wish to take the side trip, turn sharply left onto the blue-on-white-blazed Blue Disc Trail, which heads steeply uphill on a woods road. About halfway up, it turns right, leaving the road, and crosses a stream.

View from Almost Perpendicular

It then climbs even more steeply over rocks, reaching the top of Almost Perpendicular – a dramatic viewpoint from the top of a cliff – in 0.3 mile. You can see Seven Lakes Drive directly below, with the Ramapo Mountains in the background. This is another good place to stop for lunch or a short break to enjoy the spectacular views. Return as you came, watching closely for the white-blazed Kakiat Trail to join from the right. The two trails run concurrently for a short distance, and when they diverge, you should bear left, following the white blazes of the Kakiat Trail.

Return Trip: From the intersection of the Blue Disc Trail with the white-blazed Kakiat Trail, continue ahead on the Kakiat Trail for 0.6 mile. On the way, you'll cross the gas pipeline, descend through hemlocks, cross Spring Brook and its tributaries, and ascend briefly to meet the White Bar Trail (a woods road/telephone cable right-of-way) at 4.3 miles (4.9 miles if you took the Almost Perpendicular side trip). Turn right onto the White Bar Trail, marked by horizontal white blazes (and the letters "W-B" at intersections), and follow it for 0.3 mile gently downhill to the Johnsontown Road Circle, where the hike began. 🥾

Chapter 8 Almost Perpendicular and Claudius Smith Den

Shorter Hike

Rating:	**Moderate**
Distance:	**5.5 miles**
Hiking Time:	**3.25 hours**
Attractions:	**Several panoramic viewpoints from rock ledges and the historic Claudius Smith Den**
Lowest Elevation:	**380 feet**
Highest Elevation:	**1,030 feet**
Total Elevation Gain:	**1,315 feet**

Longer Hike

Rating:	**Moderate**
Distance:	**6.7 miles**
Hiking Time:	**3.75 hours**
Attractions:	**Several panoramic viewpoints from rock ledges, the historic Claudius Smith Den, and a natural rock dam**
Lowest Elevation:	**380 feet**
Highest Elevation:	**1,100 feet**
Total Elevation Gain:	**1,705 feet**
Parking GPS Coordinates:	**41.19601, -74.18404**
Map:	**NY-NJ TC Southern Harriman-Bear Mountain Trails – Map #118**

Access: Take N.J. Route 17 north to the New York State Thruway and take the first exit, Exit 15A (Sloatsburg). Turn left at the bottom of the ramp onto N.Y. Route 17 north, and continue for 4.9 miles, passing through the villages of Sloatsburg and Tuxedo. Just past the Tuxedo railroad station, turn right onto East Village Road, cross the tracks and turn left into a commuter parking lot (free parking on weekends; $2 parking fee on weekdays).

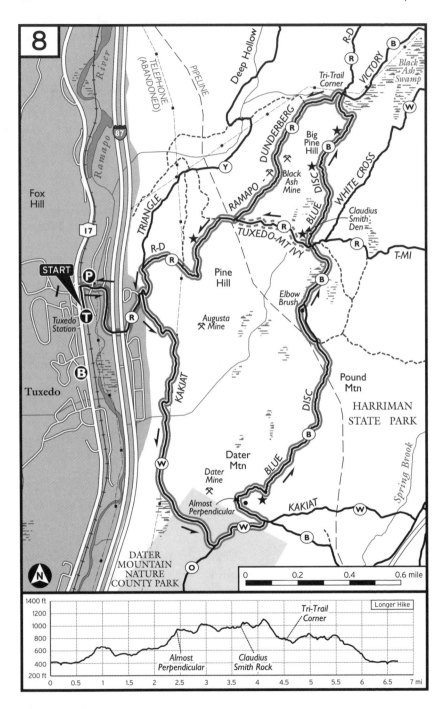

Since the hike begins at the Tuxedo railroad station, it is readily accessible by public transportation. Take the Metro-North Port Jervis Line from Hoboken or Penn Station, New York (change at Secaucus Junction) to the Tuxedo station (for more information as to fares and schedules, go to www.mta.info).

Description: If you arrived by car, walk back to the entrance to the parking lot and turn left onto East Village Road. (If you came by train, walk to the north end of the station platform, continue on the sidewalk to East Village Road, and turn right.) Proceed east on East Village Road, marked with the red-dot-on-white blazes of the Ramapo-Dunderberg (R-D) Trail, which crosses the Ramapo River and bears right to parallel the New York State Thruway. After bearing left and crossing under the Thruway, East Village Road ends at Grove Drive. Turn left on Grove Drive and follow it for 800 feet to a concrete catch basin on the right, where the road curves left. No parking is allowed here. Turn right (facing the woods) and you will see, on your right, three white blazes which mark the start of the Kakiat Trail. You will follow this trail for the next 1.5 miles.

Leave the paved road and the R-D Trail and follow the white-blazed Kakiat Trail uphill to the right, along a woods road. The trail climbs to a shoulder of the hill, then bears right and levels off on another woods road, with views of the village of Tuxedo below to the right.

About half a mile from Grove Drive, the trail descends to cross a stream. After following rock outcrops, it joins another woods road that bears left and curves around the foot of Dater Mountain, crossing into Rockland County (the county boundary is marked by a small concrete monument on the right). You'll notice many huge stone blocks which have fallen from cliffs to the left.

About 1.8 miles from the start of the hike, the Orange Trail, which leads into Dater Mountain Nature County Park, begins on the right, but you should turn left to continue along the Kakiat Trail. A quarter mile beyond the Orange Trail, soon after passing a large boulder on the right, turn left onto the Blue Disc Trail, marked by blue-dot-on-white blazes (do not turn right onto the joint Kakiat/ Blue Disc Trail).

The Blue Disc Trail leads uphill, steeply in places, to the top of Almost Perpendicular at 2.4 miles. This is a good place to stop for lunch and to enjoy the spectacular views. When you're ready to continue, follow the Blue Disc Trail north along the ridge, crossing over rock slabs, and descend into a hollow. After traversing the hollow, turn right at a huge boulder and climb steeply to the summit of Pound Mountain, which is open except for a few white pine, chestnut oak and black birch trees. At 3.0 miles, you'll cross the route of a gas pipeline, then parallel it for a short distance.

View from Almost Perpendicular

In another 750 feet, the trail splits. The "easy route," marked by a sign, goes to the right on a level path along the top of the cliffs. The main route of the Blue Disc Trail continues downhill, crosses a woods road and a stream, and turns right, following along the base of a ledge and passing through a crevice known as "Elbow Brush." Both routes rejoin near a small rock cave on the left (although you may not notice the cave if you follow the "easy" upper route). The Blue Disc Trail was once routed through the cave, and old blazes can be seen inside. The trail then parallels a stream on the left and passes a wetland.

After climbing, first gradually, then rather steeply, you'll reach an intersection with the red-dash-on-white-blazed Tuxedo-Mt. Ivy (T-MI) Trail at 3.65 miles. You must now decide whether you will take the shorter 5.5-mile hike or the longer 6.7-mile hike.

Elbow Brush

Shorter hike: Continue on the Blue Disc Trail for 250 feet, climbing to the top of Claudius Smith Rock – a beautiful formation of light-colored rock, with excellent views of the hills above Sloatsburg and Tuxedo, and of Sterling Forest beyond. After taking in the views, retrace your steps to the junction with the T-MI Trail, and turn right (west) onto this red-dash-on-white-blazed trail, which descends to the base of Claudius Smith Rock. You'll soon pass the caves known as Claudius Smith Den – one of the hideouts of Claudius Smith and his gang of thieves during the 1770s.

Claudius Smith (1736-1779) was a notorious outlaw during the American Revolution. He led a gang of thieves, consisting of his sons and several other men, known locally as the "cowboys." They robbed farms, hijacked the arsenal trains of the Continental Army, and hid out in remote caves, such as Claudius Smith Den. Smith was captured and jailed in 1777, but he escaped. In December 1778, he was captured once again, and he was hanged in Goshen, N.Y. in January 1779. Two of his sons were subsequently captured and hanged, while the third died in jail of wounds inflicted by soldiers of the Continental Army.

Continue ahead on the T-MI Trail, which skirts wetlands and descends to a junction with the red-dot-on-white-blazed R-D Trail. You have now gone 4.1 miles from the start of the hike. Turn left on the R-D Trail and begin following the directions in the section entitled "Final descent for both hikes," below.

View from the top of Claudius Smith Rock

Longer hike: Turn left on the red-dash-on-white-blazed T-MI Trail, which descends to the base of Claudius Smith Rock. In 250 feet, you'll reach the caves known as Claudius Smith Den – one of the hideouts of Claudius Smith and his gang of thieves during the 1770s (for additional information on Claudius Smith and his "gang," see the description of the "Shorter hike," above). After checking out this interesting feature, retrace your steps to the junction with the Blue Disc Trail, turn left onto this trail, and climb 250 feet to the top of Claudius Smith Rock – a beautiful formation of light-colored rock, with excellent views of the hills above Sloatsburg and Tuxedo, and of Sterling Forest beyond.

After taking in the view, continue north on the Blue Disc Trail, which descends over slabs of bare rock and passes to the right of a stand of young birch trees. Next, it climbs Big Pine Hill, with 360° views, and descends steeply over sloping rocks (use care if the rocks are wet or covered with ice). Near the base of the descent, the Blue Disc Trail turns sharply left and, at 4.55 miles, crosses a natural rock

Claudius Smith Rock, with Claudius Smith Den at its base

dam over the outflow of Black Ash Swamp to end at Tri-Trail Corner, where it meets the R-D (red dot on white) and Victory (blue "V" on white) Trails.

Turn left and follow the red-dot-on-white-blazed R-D Trail, which recrosses the outflow of Black Ash Swamp on rocks, bears right and heads downhill on a woods road. Soon, it turns left and climbs on a footpath. Near the top, it joins a woods road, passing mine pits on either side of the trail. Just before arriving at the wide gas pipeline

Hiker at the viewpoint over the village of Tuxedo from the R-D Trail

clearing, you'll pass the trailhead of the T-MI Trail on the left. To continue, follow the directions in the section entitled "Final descent for both hikes," below.

Final descent for both hikes: Follow the R-D Trail, which crosses the gas pipeline (popular with grazing deer) and climbs to a viewpoint over the village of Tuxedo. The R-D Trail now descends, steeply in places, to reach Grove Drive, 0.8 mile from the gas pipeline crossing. Turn left onto Grove Drive, then right onto East Village Road, and follow it back to the parking lot where the hike began. 🥾

Chapter 9 Ledges and Lakes

Rating:	**Strenuous**
Distance:	**8.85 miles**
Hiking Time:	**4 to 4.5 hours**
Attractions:	**Two scenic lakes, panoramic views, Dutch Doctor Shelter and the historic Claudius Smith Den**
Lowest Elevation:	**380 feet**
Highest Elevation:	**1,135 feet**
Total Elevation Gain:	**2,140 feet**
Parking GPS Coordinates:	**41.19601, -74.18404**
Map:	**NY-NJ TC Southern Harriman-Bear Mountain Trails – Map #118**

Access: Take N.J. Route 17 north to the New York State Thruway and take the first exit, Exit 15A (Sloatsburg). Turn left at the bottom of the ramp onto N.Y. Route 17 north, and continue for 4.9 miles, passing through the villages of Sloatsburg and Tuxedo. Just past the Tuxedo railroad station, turn right onto East Village Road, cross the tracks and turn left into a commuter parking lot (free parking on weekends; $2 parking fee on weekdays).

Since the hike begins at the Tuxedo railroad station, it is readily accessible by public transportation. Take the Metro-North Port Jervis Line from Hoboken or Penn Station, New York (change at Secaucus Junction) to the Tuxedo station (for more information as to fares and schedules, go to www.mta.info).

Description: If you arrived by car, walk back to the entrance to the parking lot and turn left onto East Village Road. (If you came by train, walk to the north end of the station platform, continue on the sidewalk to East Village Road, and turn right.) Proceed east on East Village Road, marked with the red-dot-on-white

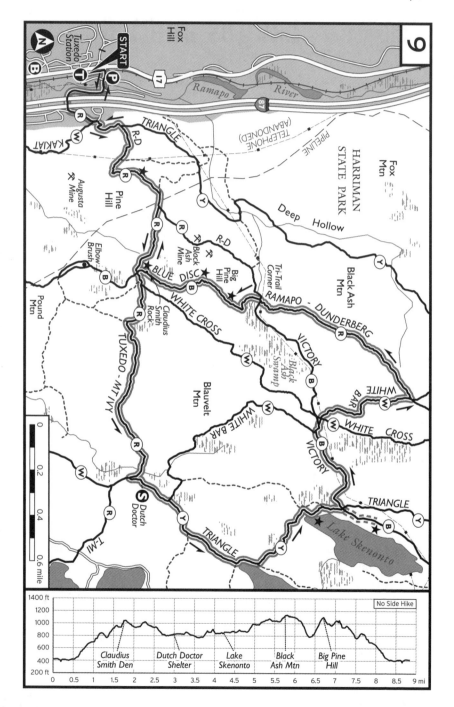

blazes of the Ramapo-Dunderberg (R-D) Trail, which crosses the Ramapo River and bears right to parallel the New York State Thruway. After bearing left and crossing under the Thruway, East Village Road ends at Grove Drive. Turn left on Grove Drive and follow it for 800 feet to a concrete catch basin on the right, where the road curves left. No parking is allowed here.

Turn right, facing the woods, and you will see two trails. The white-blazed Kakiat Trail begins on the right, but you should follow the R-D Trail, which enters the woods on the left and zigzags uphill through a forest of witch hazel, maple, beech and oak. In half a mile, it reaches a viewpoint on the left over the village of Tuxedo. After enjoying the view, continue ahead on the trail, which descends to cross the route of a gas pipeline (a good place to spot grazing deer). On the opposite side of the pipeline, the red-dash-on-white-blazed Tuxedo-Mt. Ivy (T-MI) Trail begins on the right. Turn right onto the T-MI Trail, which climbs through mixed hardwoods and past a small wetland to reach Claudius Smith Den – one of the hideouts of Claudius Smith and his gang of thieves during the 1770s.

Claudius Smith (1736-1779) was a notorious outlaw during the American Revolution. He led a gang of thieves, consisting of his sons and several other men, known locally as the "cowboys." They robbed farms, hijacked the arsenal trains of the Continental Army, and hid out in remote caves, such as Claudius Smith Den.

Dutch Doctor Shelter

Lake Sebago

Smith was captured and jailed in 1777, but he escaped. In December 1778, he was captured once again, and he was hanged in Goshen, N.Y. in January 1779. Two of his sons were subsequently captured and hanged, while the third died in jail of wounds inflicted by soldiers of the Continental Army.

As you proceed ahead along the T-MI Trail, you'll pass beneath overhanging rocks, some of which show signs of exfoliation and seem as if they could fall at any minute. This overhang can serve as a natural shelter from rain, snow or wind. Soon, you'll cross the Blue Disc Trail and pass the southern terminus of the White Cross Trail, but continue to follow the T-MI Trail, which descends to loop around a wetland (at times, this wetland can be teeming with birds). You are now 2.1 miles into the hike. Climb through a rocky area on the shoulder of Blauvelt Mountain, then begin a gradual descent, passing some folded rock outcrops along the way. Just after crossing several branches of Spring Brook, you'll reach a woods road – the route of the White Bar Trail (white horizontal blazes). You've gone 0.85 mile from the wetland and are now 2.95 miles from the start of the hike.

Turn sharply left onto the White Bar Trail (do not follow the joint T-MI/White Bar Trail straight ahead). On your right, about 300 feet from the junction, the Dutch Doctor Shelter – a good place to escape the elements if the weather is bad – is on a rise to your right. After just 0.2 mile on the White Bar Trail, you'll reach the start of the Triangle Trail, marked by three yellow triangles. Here, the White Bar Trail turns left, but you should continue straight ahead, following the Triangle Trail.

As you proceed along the Triangle Trail, the vegetation changes from a hardwood forest to a pretty stretch of mountain laurel. In about half a mile, just after passing the second of two unmarked trails on the right that lead to ADK's Camp Nawakwa, the Triangle Trail reaches the shore of Lake Sebago and crosses a tiny inlet on rocks. It follows the shoreline for a short distance, then turns left and climbs over two small ridges. After turning right onto a woods road and crossing the inlet of Lake Skenonto (which is now on your right), the trail suddenly turns right onto a rock slab and follows the shore of the lake. You are now about 4.2 miles into the hike. In another 250 feet, a woods road on the right leads to a beautiful viewpoint over the lake. A short distance beyond, you'll reach an intersection with the Victory Trail – a woods road marked with a blue "V" on a white background. Turn left (southwest) onto the Victory Trail.

Lunch break option: If you wish to take a lunch break, turn right (northeast) rather than left on the Victory Trail. Soon, you will come to a secluded viewpoint over the lake, with large boulders overlooking the water on your right. After enjoying your break, retrace your steps on the Victory Trail. When you reach the intersection with the Triangle Trail, continue straight ahead (southwest) on the Victory Trail. This optional side trip adds 0.4 mile to the hike.

JASON HARCSZTARK

Lake Skenonto

After crossing and then recrossing a power/telephone line and passing by wetlands, the Victory Trail reaches an intersection with the White Bar Trail, which briefly joins from the left, as the Victory Trail curves to the right. When the two trails split in another 200 feet, bear right, continuing to follow the White Bar Trail, which immediately crosses the White Cross Trail, goes under the power/telephone lines, and proceeds uphill through stands of blueberry bushes, mountain laurel, maple, chestnut oak and white pine.

After half a mile on the White Bar Trail, you'll reach an intersection with the red-dot-on-white-blazed R-D Trail. You've now gone a total of 5.35 miles (not counting the lunch break side trip). Turn left onto the R-D Trail, which descends, crosses a wet area and climbs up a bedrock slab to the top of Black Ash Mountain. This area is especially beautiful in the fall, and the views are excellent. After a short, steep downhill scramble, you'll pass numerous glacial erratics and descend more steeply, cross under power lines and reach the edge of Black Ash Swamp at 6.3 miles. This spot is known as Tri-Trail Corner because three trails – R-D, Victory, and Blue Disc – intersect.

The R-D Trail turns right here, but you should bear left and follow the blue-dot-on-white-blazed Blue Disc Trail, which crosses the outlet of Black Ash Swamp on large rock slabs and begins a steep but scenic climb through hemlock, chestnut oak, birch, cedar, moss and ferns. After crossing slabs of bedrock, the trail reaches the summit of Big Pine Hill, marked by a rock cairn, with 360° views. To the right

Blue Disc Trail along Black Ash Swamp

DAN BALOGH

North-facing view from Big Pine Hill

(west), you can clearly see Orange County's highest point, Schunemunk Mountain, where Claudius Smith's gang was chased and his son William was mortally wounded by the Continental Army.

Continue on the Blue Disc Trail as it makes a short, steep descent and then a brief ascent to the top of Claudius Smith Rock – a beautiful formation of light-colored rock, with excellent views of the hills above Sloatsburg and Tuxedo, and of Sterling Forest beyond. After taking in the views, continue along the Blue Disc Trail for another 250 feet, descending to a junction with the red-dash-on-white-blazed T-MI Trail. This intersection, partway down the rocks, is easy to miss. Turn right onto the T-MI Trail. You will now be retracing your steps along the T-MI and R-D Trail back to the start of the hike.

Be careful on the short, steep descent to the base of Claudius Smith Rock. Continue downhill on the T-MI Trail to its terminus at the R-D Trail, 7.45 miles from the start of the hike. Turn left onto the R-D Trail, cross the gas pipeline, climb to the viewpoint over the village of Tuxedo, and descend to Grove Drive. Turn left onto Grove Drive, then turn right onto East Village Road and follow it back to the parking area at the Tuxedo railroad station, where the hike began. 🏃

Chapter 10 **Parker Cabin Mountain**

Rating:	**Moderate to strenuous**
Distance:	**5.0 miles**
Hiking Time:	**3 hours**
Attractions:	**Five summits, 1,640 vertical feet of climbing, and views of Lakes Stahahe, Sebago and Kanawauke, as well as Little Long Pond**
Lowest Elevation:	**690 feet**
Highest Elevation:	**1,290 feet**
Total Elevation Gain:	**1,640 feet**
Parking GPS Coordinates:	**41.23488, -74.14906**
Map:	**NY-NJ TC Southern Harriman-Bear Mountain Trails – Map #118**

Access: Take N.J. Route 17 north to the New York State Thruway and take the first exit, Exit 15A (Sloatsburg). Turn left at the bottom of the ramp onto N.Y. Route 17 north, and continue through the villages of Sloatsburg and Tuxedo. About 2.2 miles beyond the village of Tuxedo, bear left at a traffic light at the intersection of N.Y. Route 17A. At the top of the ramp, turn right onto County Route 106 (Kanawauke Road), crossing over Route 17 and then going under the New York State Thruway. Continue for about 2.2 miles to the first parking area on the right side of the road. The parking area, which is past Lake Stahahe (visible through trees to the left), is just beyond a sharp curve in the road.

Description: From the western edge of the parking area, follow the horizontal white blazes of the White Bar Trail uphill, heading southwest (do not cross Route 106). As the trail climbs to the northern summit of Car Pond Mountain, it passes a shallow vernal pool and curves to the right. Just before the trail curves to the left and begins to descend, you may wish to continue straight ahead for 100 feet

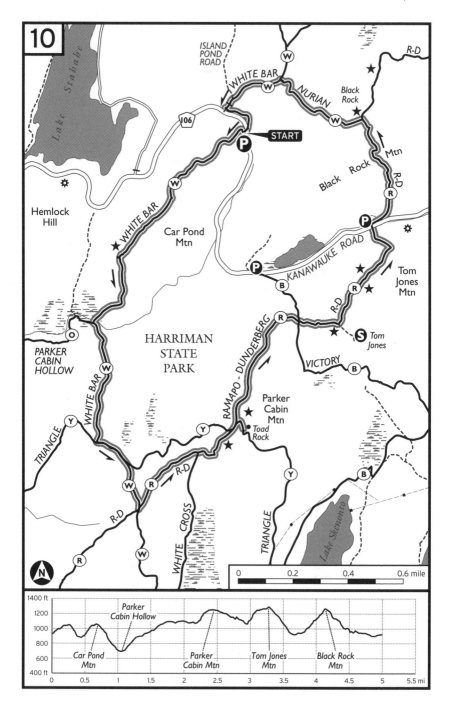

View from the glacial erratic along the R-D Trail near the summit of Parker Cabin Mountain

to a seasonal off-trail view to the northwest over Lake Stahahe, with Stahahe High Peak visible behind it and the hills of Sterling Forest in the distance.

After taking in the view, return to the White Bar Trail, bear right, and descend steeply through a mixed hardwood forest into a hollow. The trail now climbs the southern peak of Car Pond Mountain, passing just west of the summit. As the trail begins to descend, you will reach a second, more open viewpoint from a rock ledge just to the right of the trail. From here, you can see a number of peaks in Harriman State Park and Sterling Forest.

The White Bar Trail now descends into Parker Cabin Hollow. About a mile into the hike, it crosses a stream on a wooden bridge and reaches a T-intersection. This is the lowest point of the hike. The orange-blazed Parker Cabin Hollow Trail begins on the right, but you should turn left to continue on the White Bar Trail. This hollow once was the site of a cabin belonging to a horse thief named Parker, who was killed there by Tom Jones, a member of Claudius Smith's gang.

The White Bar Trail now ascends steadily on a woods road. At 1.5 miles, the yellow-blazed Triangle Trail joins from the right. Turn left and continue on the joint White Bar/Triangle Trail. In another 0.15 mile, bear right to stay on the

White Bar Trail, as the Triangle Trail leaves to the left. In 0.2 mile, you'll reach another T-intersection just below the top of the ridge, where you should turn left onto the red-dot-on-white-blazed Ramapo-Dunderberg (R-D) Trail. You have now hiked 1.85 miles, and you will be following the R-D Trail for the next 2.3 miles.

The R-D Trail now descends slightly. In 0.3 mile, the White Cross Trail begins on the right, and the R-D makes a short, steep ascent up Parker Cabin Mountain. At the top of the steep climb, by a glacial erratic, you'll reach a panoramic viewpoint from a rock ledge over Black Ash Swamp and the surrounding mountains. After taking some time to enjoy the view, continue along the R-D Trail to the summit of the mountain. Here, the yellow-blazed Triangle Trail joins briefly, then leaves to the right. When the two trails split, you should turn right and continue along the Triangle Trail for 100 feet to another viewpoint from a rock ledge, with Lake Sebago visible to the right. Just below the ledge, you can see "Toad Rock" – a boulder that perfectly resembles a toad (this feature was named by Bob Fuller in 1966). After taking in the view, retrace your steps to the Triangle/R-D junction and turn right, now following the red-dot-on-white blazes of the R-D Trail heading north. You have now hiked 2.45 miles.

The trail continues along the semi-open ridge, passing a small vernal pool and descending over bare slabs of rock. In about half a mile, you'll cross the Victory Trail, marked with blue-"V"-on-white blazes, with an old stone fireplace

Toad Rock

Tom Jones Shelter

on your right. The R-D Trail now steeply climbs Tom Jones Mountain, named after the one who murdered Parker. At the top of the steep climb, an unmarked trail to the right leads to the Tom Jones Shelter – an excellent spot for a lunch break or to temporarily escape the elements (the shelter is not visible from the trail). Continue to ascend more gradually to the summit, reached at 3.3 miles, with great views to the east of Jackie Jones Mountain, distinguishable by its massive communications towers and relatively small-looking fire tower to the right.

Follow the R-D Trail as it descends to the northeast, with Black Rock Mountain, Little Long Pond and Lake Kanawauke visible ahead as you descend. The switchbacks on the way down are steep and often eroded, so walk carefully. At the base of the descent, the trail crosses Route 106 (Kanawauke Road) by two small parking areas at 3.7 miles. It briefly turns right and parallels the road, then turns left just before a guardrail, crosses a brook and bears left into the woods.

Soon, the R-D Trail begins to climb Black Rock Mountain, passing huge boulders and lichen-covered cliffs along the way. In half a mile, it reaches the bare rock summit at a junction with the vertical-white-blazed Nurian Trail. Turn left, leaving the R-D Trail, and follow the Nurian Trail to the very top of the ridge, with impressive 360° views. Stahahe High Peak and Car Pond Mountain are visible to the west, and Parker Cabin and Tom Jones Mountains to the south

North-facing view from the Nurian Trail on Black Rock Mountain

(you just climbed three of these four peaks!). After taking in the great views, follow the Nurian Trail steeply downhill over rocks and across a small brook. Watch for snakes in this area. After crossing the brook, climb briefly to reach a woods road – the route of the White Bar Trail (note that the White Bar's white blazes are horizontal, while the Nurian Trail's are vertical).

Turn left onto the White Bar Trail, which descends gradually, crosses a small brook on a culvert, then turns left to parallel Route 106 (Kanawauke Road). The trail soon crosses Route 106, returning you to the parking area where the hike began. 🚶

Chapter 11   **Breakneck Mountain**

Rating:	**Moderate**
Distance:	**7.1 miles (7.7 miles with optional side hike)**
Hiking Time:	**4 hours (4.5 hours with optional side hike)**
Attractions:	**Glacial erratics on open rock slabs, views of Breakneck Pond and Third Reservoir, long stands of mountain laurel**
Lowest Elevation:	**425 feet**
Highest Elevation:	**1,260 feet**
Total Elevation Gain:	**1,455 feet (1,625 feet with optional side hike)**
Parking GPS Coordinates:	**41.18512, -74.07453**
Map:	**NY-NJ TC Southern Harriman- Bear Mountain Trails – Map #118**

This hike explores a relatively quiet section of southeastern Harriman State Park, following the Tuxedo-Mt. Ivy, Breakneck Mountain, Suffern-Bear Mountain, and Red Arrow Trails. The hike takes you through deep woods, including a long stand of dense mountain laurel. The Breakneck Mountain section traverses open rock slabs with interesting rock formations and includes some views of Breakneck Pond. The steepest and rockiest parts are at the beginning and end of the hike; here, the Trail Conference has rerouted steep, eroded sections of the Tuxedo-Mt. Ivy Trail, which has greatly improved the hiking experience. Overall, the trails are not difficult, and the atmosphere is peaceful.

Access: Take the Palisades Interstate Parkway north to Exit 13 (U.S. 202/ Suffern/Haverstraw). Turn right at the bottom of the ramp onto U.S. 202 west, and proceed 1.7 miles to a junction with N.Y. 306. Turn right onto Old Route 306, then right again at the stop sign just ahead. In 0.2 mile, turn left onto Mountain Road (at a sign for "Ramaquois"), then, in another 0.2 mile, turn left again onto Diltzes Lane. Follow Diltzes Lane for 0.2 mile and, immediately after crossing

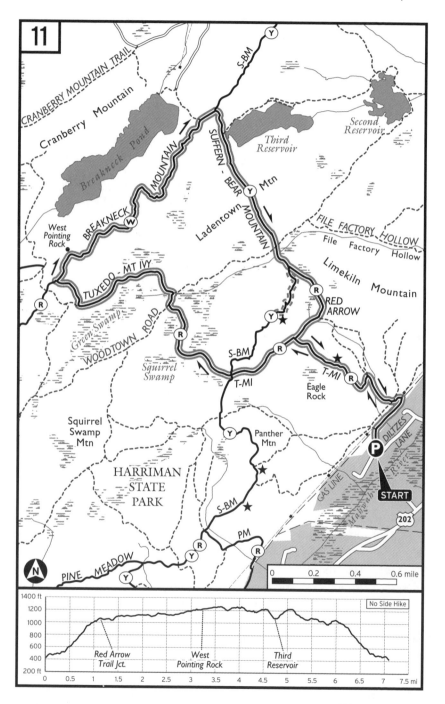

some small speed bumps, turn right into a gravel parking area with a sign indicating that parking for hikers is available.

Description: At the left rear corner of the parking area, at a green gate that blocks off the power line access road, find the triple-red-dash-on-white blaze that marks the start of the Tuxedo-Mt. Ivy (T-MI) Trail. Follow this trail uphill on a wide dirt road (used to access the nearby power lines). Bear right as you approach the power lines and continue along the dirt road, which runs parallel to the power lines. After crossing two small streams and passing the next power line tower, bear left, under the power lines, to a Y-junction at a black chain-link fence. Here you should take the left fork and continue uphill, still following the T-MI Trail. In a short distance, the trail turns right, leaving the service road, and heads into the woods. Immediately after the turn, there are two unofficial trails heading off to the right, but you should continue straight ahead on the T-MI Trail.

The trail ascends gradually on a rocky woods road, bordered for part of the way by the remnants of stone walls. After crossing a stream on rocks, watch for a sudden left turn, and follow the T-MI Trail as it leaves one woods road and begins to follow another. The trail now climbs more steeply. Near the top of the climb, it bears right and continues on a footpath. Just below the summit of Eagle Rock, keep a close eye out for a limited view, which will briefly open up over your right shoulder. From here you can see Limekiln Mountain to the north, the Hudson River to the east, and High Tor in the distance to the southeast. High Tor is part

Viewpoint on the T-MI Trail

of the northern Palisades and is traversed by the 356-mile-long Long Path, the second longest trail in Harriman, which runs from the George Washington Bridge through Harriman State Park and north to the foothills of the Adirondacks.

Continuing past the viewpoint, the trail climbs more gradually and soon reaches a T-junction. The Red Arrow Trail, which will be your return route, begins on the right, but you should turn left to continue on the T-MI Trail, which now descends gently past a seasonally wet area. After two brief climbs, you will cross the yellow-blazed Suffern-Bear Mountain Trail at the high point of the land. This junction is marked by an interesting rock outcrop on the right and an old stone fireplace and a small hollow on the left. The 23-mile-long Suffern-Bear Mountain Trail runs the length of Harriman-Bear Mountain Parks, from the village of Suffern in western Rockland County to the foot of Bear Mountain, near the Hudson River. Proposed in 1924 by Major William A. Welch, then general manager of the Palisades Interstate Park Commission, it is the longest trail in the park. You will be following a portion of the S-BM Trail later on in the hike, but for now, continue ahead on the T-MI Trail.

The T-MI Trail levels off and passes through beautiful stands of mountain laurel, which will seem to envelop you for next mile of your hike. In about half a mile, the trail reaches a T-junction with Woodtown Road, a woods road. It turns right and follows the road, crosses a stream on a small wooden footbridge, and immediately leaves the road and turns sharply left onto another old woods road, still lined with colorful mountain laurels.

Along the Breakneck Mountain Trail

West Pointing Rock

The trail begins to climb and soon crosses a small stream on rocks. It then passes by a wetland known as the Green Swamp on the left. The mountain laurels are soon replaced by a hardwood forest. Watch carefully, just beyond another short climb, for the T-MI Trail to turn right, leaving the woods road it has been following. A short distance beyond, keep an eye out for the next junction, marked with three plain white blazes on a tree and the letters "BM" painted on a rock. Here, you should leave the T-MI Trail and turn right on the white-blazed Breakneck Mountain Trail. You have now hiked 3.1 miles.

Breakneck Mountain was once known locally as Knapp Mountain after the name of the original owner. The Breakneck Mountain Trail is not to be confused with the extremely steep and wildly popular Breakneck Ridge Trail, on the east side of the Hudson River, near Cold Spring, N.Y. The Breakneck Mountain Trail, also built at the suggestion of Major Welch, follows a long ridgeline that features glacial erractics, open rock slabs and several views of Breakneck Pond below.

Continuing on the trail, you will soon reach West Pointing Rock, a 10-by-14-foot boulder with a sharp, westward-pointing projection. Next, you'll cross several open slabs, some with large boulders left by the glacier that once covered this area. If you keep an eye to the left, you will eventually catch glimpses of Breakneck Pond, especially if you hike the trail when the leaves are down.

In 1.5 miles, the white-blazed Breakneck Mountain Trail ends at a Y-junction with the yellow-blazed Suffern-Bear Mountain (S-BM) Trail. Look carefully, as the yellow blazes lead in two opposite directions here. Do not turn left (up the rocks), but instead continue straight ahead, following the yellow blazes downhill and to the right. You've now hiked a total of 4.6 miles.

You will soon reach the western end of the Third Reservoir, a beautiful spot for a rest or lunch break. Built in 1951, the Third Reservoir is the newest of the three reservoirs built to serve the now-closed Letchworth Village State Developmental Center. Even with three reservoirs, Letchworth Village used to run out of water in dry years, and when this happened, a pipe was laid over Breakneck Mountain and water pumped out of Breakneck Pond.

From the Third Reservoir, the S-BM Trail climbs over Ladentown Mountain and descends to Woodtown Road. It crosses the road and a stream and climbs to a junction with the Red Arrow Trail, 5.5 miles from the start of the hike (the junction is marked by cairns). To finish your hike promptly, turn left on the Red Arrow Trail and skip ahead one paragraph.

Along the Breakneck Mountain Trail

DAN BALOGH

DAN BALOGH

Third Reservoir

Optional Side Trip: If you have time and want to take in another view, do not turn left on the Red Arrow Trail; instead, continue straight ahead on the yellow-blazed S-BM Trail for another 0.3 mile. The trail takes you uphill to a bird's-eye view of the Hudson River valley. After enjoying the view, turn around and follow the yellow trail back downhill, keeping a close eye out for the Red Arrow Trail junction, where you should turn right.

The Red Arrow Trail skirts the edge of a swamp and descends past some old rock walls and through mountain laurel thickets. Pay attention as the trail bears right at a fork, then bears right again and continues uphill, now following a woods road. Soon, you'll reach the end of the Red Arrow Trail, marked by a triple blaze. Turn left onto the Tuxedo-Mt. Ivy Trail (red dash on white) and follow it downhill, noting that you followed this trail up the mountain at the beginning of your hike. Once again, you will pass a viewpoint over the Hudson River valley on your left. Continue following the red-dash-on-white blazes downhill to your car, retracing the same route you followed at the start of the hike. 🥾

Chapter 12   **Boston Mine and Stahahe High Peak**

Rating:	**Strenuous**
Distance:	**6.5 miles (7.5 miles with side trip to Stahahe High Peak)**
Hiking Time:	**4.5 hours (5.5 hours with side trip to Stahahe High Peak)**
Attractions:	**Views from Black Rock, Surebridge Mountain and Stahahe High Peak, an interesting mine and a secluded pond**
Lowest Elevation:	**900 feet**
Highest Elevation:	**1,382 feet**
Total Elevation Gain:	**1,395 feet (1,650 feet with optional side trip to Stahahe High Peak)**
Parking GPS Coordinates:	**41.23488, -74.14906**
Map:	**NY-NJ TC Northern Harriman-Bear Mountain Trails – Map #119**

Access: Take N.J. Route 17 north to the New York State Thruway and take the first exit, Exit 15A (Sloatsburg). Turn left at the bottom of the ramp onto N.Y. Route 17 north, and continue through the villages of Sloatsburg and Tuxedo. About 2.2 miles beyond the village of Tuxedo, bear left at a traffic light at the intersection of N.Y. Route 17A. At the top of the ramp, turn right onto Route 106 (Kanawauke Road), crossing over Route 17 and then going under the New York State Thruway. Continue for about 2.2 miles to the first parking area on the right side of the road. The parking area, which is past Lake Stahahe (visible through trees to the left), is just beyond a sharp curve in the road.

Description: From the western edge of parking area, follow the horizontal white rectangular blazes of the White Bar Trail north across Route 106 (Kanawauke Road). The trail curves left and descends slightly. After paralleling Route 106 for a short distance, it turns right on a woods road and crosses over a

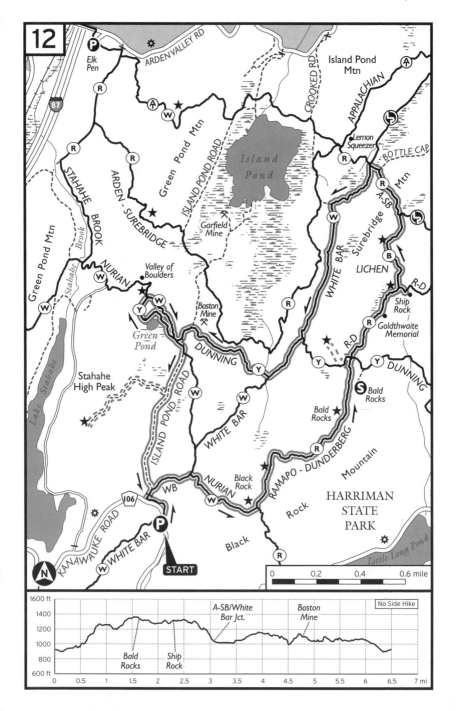

stream. A short distance beyond, you'll reach a fork in the road. The left branch is Island Pond Road, which will be your return route, but you should bear right and continue to follow the White Bar Trail. The trail ascends gently through a mixed hardwood forest for a quarter mile before meeting another white-blazed trail, the Nurian Trail. (Both trails are blazed white, but the Nurian blazes are vertical rather than horizontal). Turn right and follow the Nurian Trail downhill into the hemlocks, crossing a tiny stream on rocks. Evergreens give way to hardwoods and rock formations as you make a 300-foot vertical climb up Black Rock Mountain. Non-venomous black rat snakes have been seen on this stretch of the Nurian Trail, so keep an eye out.

In 0.8 mile (from the start of the hike), you'll reach the top of Black Rock Mountain, with its panoramic 360° views. To the south, you can see Tom Jones and Parker Cabin Mountains; to the west, Car Pond Mountain and Stahahe High Peak are visible. A few steps further, the Nurian Trail ends at a T-intersection with the red-dot-on-white-blazed Ramapo-Dunderberg (R-D) Trail. Turn left on the R-D Trail and begin a beautiful walk on bare, exposed granite ledges, with vernal ponds visible below. After dipping into a pretty hollow, you'll climb past large glacial boulders to Bald Rocks. Due to the lack of trees along this section of the trail, many blazes are painted on the bedrock below your feet (navigation can be challenging here when the ground is snow-covered). At 1,382 feet, Bald Rocks is the highest elevation in Harriman and Bear Mountain Parks. The actual high point – marked by a U.S. Coast and Geodetic Survey marker – is a short distance off trail to the left and offers a panoramic west-facing view. You've now gone 1.65 miles from the start of the hike.

West-facing view from Bald Rocks

A short distance beyond the summit, you'll pass the Bald Rocks Shelter, which is visible below on your right. Continue along the R-D Trail, which descends to cross the yellow-blazed Dunning Trail. If you'd like to take a short side trip to another viewpoint, turn left onto the Dunning Trail. In a short distance, you'll notice a cairn marking the start of a distinct unmarked trail that leads to the right. Follow this trail up to another high point (about 1,340 feet in elevation) in a secluded area, with a beautiful west-facing view, then return to the Dunning Trail, turn left, and turn left again to continue along the R-D Trail.

The R-D Trail proceeds through an open area, with a few hemlocks, white birches, white pines, pitch pines and blueberry bushes. This area was burned in a forest fire in 2000 but is now starting to regenerate. After climbing a little, you'll come to the Goldthwaite Memorial – a bronze plaque on a boulder to the right of the trail, placed by the Fresh Air Club in memory of George Goldthwaite (1889-1960), who once hiked the entire 23-mile R-D Trail in 4 hours and 51 minutes!

Bald Rocks Shelter

The trail now descends steeply to cross a small vernal pond on a log bridge, then climbs to a junction with the blue-"L"-on-white-blazed Lichen Trail, which begins on the left. Continue along the R-D Trail for about 250 feet to Ship Rock, a huge boulder which resembles the bow of a ship. After checking out this interesting feature, retrace your steps to the junction and turn right onto the Lichen Trail. This short, scenic trail goes through a fire-damaged area, offering views of Island Pond to the west, the Arden House to the northwest and part of Schunemunk Mountain (Orange County's highest point) to the north. In about half a mile, after making a winding and sometimes steep descent, the Lichen Trail ends in a hemlock forest at a junction with the red-triangle-on-white-blazed Arden-Surebridge Trail and the aqua-blazed Long Path.

Turn left onto the joint Arden-Surebridge Trail/Long Path, which passes a wet area, goes down along a tiny stream and crosses a ravine. In 0.3 mile, just before the Long Path leaves to the right, the White Bar Trail begins on the left (you may remember from earlier that its white blazes are horizontal, rather than vertical). Turn left onto this relatively wide, level trail, which leads through a wet area and into a pretty, sheltered evergreen forest. After about 0.3 mile, the White Bar Trail bears left and joins the Crooked Road – an old woods road – which begins to climb. You will cross some tiny streams and pass interesting rock formations on your left. (If you choose to run the White Bar Trail, slow down and be careful at the water crossings!)

After 0.9 mile along the White Bar Trail, just after crossing a tiny stream, the yellow-blazed Dunning Trail joins from the left, and both trails bear right. In a quarter of a mile, after crossing another stream on a natural rock bridge, the White Bar and Dunning Trails split. Turn right and follow the yellow-blazed Dunning Trail, which heads downhill and over two small ridges on a narrow footpath. In about half a mile, you will descend alongside mine tailings and reach the opening of the Boston Mine on your right. This is one of the larger and more interesting mines in Harriman State Park, with its deep L-shaped cut in the rock and water-filled mine shaft. Use caution, as the entrance to the mine is often wet.

Boston Mine

Here, the Dunning Trail turns left and, after passing more piles of tailings, it turns left again onto Island Pond Road, an unmarked woods road.

In only 500 feet, the Dunning Trail turns right, leaving Island Pond Road, and continues on a narrow footpath. It crosses the white-blazed Nurian Trail, passes a phragmites-filled wetland, and reaches the pristine Green Pond.

Green Pond

The grade steepens a little as the trail swings around the northern and western sides of the pond, passing under a huge overhanging boulder, and climbs a small hill. After a short descent, the Dunning Trail ends at a junction with the white-blazed Nurian Trail. Turn right and follow the Nurian Trail for 0.3 mile back to Island Pond Road (you will re-cross the Dunning Trail once more just before reaching the road). Although the two trails closely parallel each other, they are each quite different.

When you reach Island Pond Road, turn right. Almost immediately, the Nurian Trail leaves to the left, but you should continue ahead on the unmarked Island Pond Road. In 0.2 mile, at the precise spot where the vegetation changes from evergreens and mountain laurel to deciduous trees, a cairn marks the start of an unmarked trail on the right. If you wish to visit Stahahe High Peak (it's about a one-mile round trip), turn right and follow this trail, which leads west through mountain laurel. You may find some unofficial blue blazes along the way. The trail heads southwest past two small vernal ponds and becomes more difficult to follow as it makes its final ascent to the open rock ledges of the summit (the last section of the trail may be marked with cairns). After enjoying the view from the summit, continue a little further down the rocks, where you will find the best views of Lake Stahahe, Green Pond Mountain and Sterling Forest. Return as you came (being careful to bear right, downhill, after the first pond to avoid another

unofficial blue-blazed trail that continues north along the ridge). When you reach Island Pond Road, turn right and head south along the unmarked road.

Island Pond Road descends moderately for half a mile before joining the White Bar Trail just before Route 106 (Kanawauke Road). You are now retracing the route you followed for the first part of the hike. Continue ahead on the White Bar Trail as it crosses the stream, turns sharply left and parallels Route 106 for 0.1 mile, then crosses Route 106 and reaches the parking area where the hike began.

Lake Stahahe from Stahahe High Peak

Chapter 13 Island Pond and the Lemon Squeezer

Single Loop

Rating:	**Moderate**
Distance:	**6.6 miles**
Hiking Time:	**3.5 hours**
Lowest Elevation:	**550 feet**
Highest Elevation:	**1,200 feet**
Total Elevation Gain:	**1,655 feet**

Double Loop

Rating:	**Strenuous**
Distance:	**8.05 miles**
Hiking Time:	**4.5 hours**
Lowest Elevation:	**550 feet**
Highest Elevation:	**1,303 feet**
Total Elevation Gain:	**1,890 feet**

Attractions:	**One of Harriman's most unusual rock formations, diverse terrain and forests, scenic lake, wetlands and wildlife viewing**
Parking GPS Coordinates:	**41.26475, -74.15434**
Map:	**NY-NJ TC Northern Harriman-Bear Mountain Trails – Map #119**

Access: Take N.J. Route 17 north to the New York State Thruway and take the first exit, Exit 15A (Sloatsburg). Turn left at the bottom of the ramp onto N.Y. Route 17 north and continue through the villages of Sloatsburg, Tuxedo and Southfields. About two miles north of Southfields, turn right onto Arden Valley Road just beyond a "Welcome to Harriman State Park" sign. Cross the bridge over the New York State Thruway, then make the first right into the Elk Pen parking area.

Description: From the east side of the parking area, follow the white blazes of the Appalachian Trail (A.T.), which head eastward through a grassy meadow of milk thistle, goldenrod and raspberry bushes toward the forested hills. At the edge of the woods, the A.T. turns right onto a woods road known as Arden Road (built by Edward Harriman in 1894 to connect Arden to Southfields). Here, you

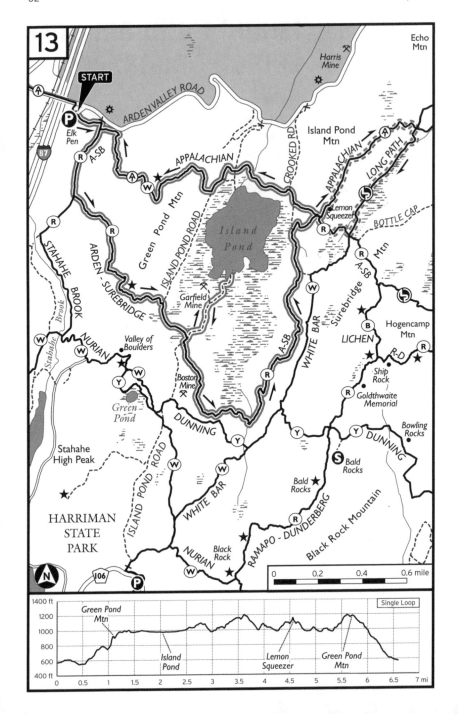

will see a triple inverted-red-triangle-on-white blaze that marks the start of the Arden-Surebridge (A-SB) Trail. Both trails run concurrently along the road. In 100 feet, the A.T. turns left, leaving Arden Road, but you should continue along the road, now following only the A-SB Trail. The road now heads gradually downhill through hemlocks and hardwoods. The field below on the right, known as the Elk Pen, was actually home to a herd of elk from Yellowstone National Park between 1919 and 1942. Rusted sections of the old iron fence are still visible.

In 0.35 mile, the Stahahe Brook Trail (red horizontal stripe on white) begins and continues ahead on Arden Road, but you should follow the inverted-red-triangle-on-white blazes of the A-SB Trail as they turn left, leaving the road. The A-SB Trail now begins a steady climb, following and then crossing a brook. It bears right and climbs less steeply, with cliffs to the left. After passing an interesting boulder on the left, the trail descends a little, bears left to cross another brook, then begins a steep climb of Green Pond Mountain. Near the top, the trail bears left, passes an overhanging rock on the right, then climbs stone steps and switches back to the right, following a narrow ledge along a precipice. This trail section can become icy in the winter, and caution should be exercised.

After climbing a little more, you'll come to a partial clearing among young fir trees at 1.1 miles. Here, an unmarked path on the left leads about 50 feet to a rock outcrop that affords a nice view of the valley below. After resting from your climb, return to the A-SB Trail and turn left. You'll pass a vernal pond on your right and continue over undulating terrain before entering stands of mountain laurel and reaching Island Pond Road, which joins from the left at 1.45 miles.

Bear right here, continuing to follow the A-SB Trail, which descends along Island Pond Road and crosses a beautiful wetland with tall grasses. One can often find evidence of bears in this area, which can be buggy in summertime and difficult to cross when water levels are high. After climbing briefly through hemlock and mountain laurel, you'll come to a triangular intersection at 1.65 miles. Take the left fork, leaving the A-SB Trail for now, and head north on an unmarked woods road. In 0.2 mile, you'll reach another fork. The left fork leads about 250 feet to several exploratory pits and a trench marking the remnants of the Garfield Mine, but you should take the right fork, which leads in 0.2 mile to the ruins of a stone cabin, built by the Park for its rangers.

Ruins of stone cabin at Island Pond

Island Pond

Just ahead, a rock outcrop offers a panoramic view of Island Pond. During a recent drought, the top of the submerged Garfield Mine became partly visible in Island Pond. (If you are intrigued with iron mines, be sure to visit nearby Boston Mine, described in Chapter 12.)

After enjoying the view, retrace your steps, following the road for 0.4 mile back to the triangular intersection. Bear left, then continue ahead to rejoin the inverted-red-triangle-on-white-blazed A-SB Trail and Island Pond Road. Follow the road for only 150 feet, and be alert for a sharp left turn at a cairn, where the A-SB Trail leaves the road. Continue to follow the A-SB Trail as it climbs a little and then descends into a valley, with a deep evergreen forest in an environment that closely resembles northern New England. After crossing an outlet stream of Island Pond, the trail begins to climb through an area punctuated by iron, quartzite and blackish pitchblende embedded in the gneiss rock, with occasional limited views of Island Pond to the left.

At the crest of the rise, you'll pass an interesting boulder perched on smaller rocks, with ferns on its top. The trail now descends through hemlocks and pines, crosses a stream, and climbs over another rise. At the base of the descent, it joins an old mining road, the "Crooked Road," which comes in from the right at 4.05 miles. The A-SB Trail now crosses a stream and climbs to a junction where it turns right, leaving the Crooked Road. It continues to climb until, at 4.45 miles, it joins the Appalachian Trail (A.T.), which comes in from the left. Bear right and follow the joint A-SB/A.T. for about 200 feet until the two trails split at the base of the fascinating rock formation known as the Lemon Squeezer, marked by two huge overhanging boulders.

Turn left and follow the A.T. under these boulders and then through a narrow passageway between rocks, where you will have to lean at a 15° angle to get through. You'll emerge beneath a massive overhanging rock, with a steep climb just ahead. You now must decide whether to continue ahead on the A.T., following the longer double loop, or to return via the shorter single loop. If you choose the single loop, retrace your steps through the Lemon Squeezer, turn right on the joint A-SB/A.T. at the base of this rock formation, and skip to the description of the "Return Route," below.

Longer Route (Double Loop): Continue ahead on the white-blazed A.T., immediately reaching a very steep climb over rocks. A sign points to an easy, blue-blazed bypass to the left, but if you choose the tougher rock scramble (the main A.T. route), consider leaning back into the main cliff for leverage as you find hand- and footholds. You may wish to toss your pack up (or hand it to a friend) so it does not encumber your scramble upward.

At the top, bear right, and continue to follow the white blazes to the top of Island Pond Mountain (elevation 1,303 feet). Just to the north of the trail, you will find the stone foundations of a summer home built by Edward Harriman. Your descent is scenic and includes long, sloped stretches of bare rock, fern-filled hollows and a deep hemlock forest near the bottom. At 5.2 miles, you'll reach a junction with the aqua blazes of the Long Path, marked by a four-tiered sign giving distances north and south along the A.T. and the Long Path. Turn sharply right onto the Long Path and follow it over large rocks and along the edge of the inappropriately-named Dismal Swamp, a wetland which adds diversity and a splash of color to the hike. To your left, you can see Surebridge Mountain across the swamp. After 0.6 mile on the Long Path, turn right, rejoining the

Lemon Squeezer

inverted-red-triangle-on-white-blazed A-SB Trail. After climbing over some large rocks, you'll reach the entrance to the Lemon Squeezer on your right at 6.05 miles. Turn left, briefly retracing your steps on the joint A-SB/A.T.

Return Route: Just ahead, where the A-SB and A.T. split, continue ahead, leaving the A-SB and following the white-blazed A.T., which descends rather steeply to rejoin the Crooked Road near the shore of Island Pond. After briefly following the Crooked Road, the A.T. turns left and climbs a knoll, with a limited view of Island Pond to the left. It descends through stands of oak, beech and maple, passes the rusted remains of a rotary gravel classifier and several piles of rock, and crosses an outlet of the pond. Here, a wooden bridge spans a stone spillway built by the Civilian Conservation Corps in the 1930s, during the Great Depression. The project, which would have increased the size of Island Pond – one of the few lakes in the Park that remains in its natural state – was never completed.

Four-tiered distances sign

At 5.15 miles (6.6 miles, if you've taken the longer double loop), you'll cross a gravel road that leads from Arden Valley Road to Island Pond. After briefly joining a woods road, the A.T. turns left and rejoins Island Pond Road. It follows the road for 400 feet, then turns right and begins to climb Green Pond Mountain, steeply in places, with the last part of the climb on stone steps. The mountain features wild blueberry bushes, wild turkey and surprisingly tame deer. On the western side of the relatively flat summit (elevation 1,180 feet), reached at 5.7 miles (7.15 miles on the double loop), rock outcrops on the right of the trail offer limited views of the Ramapo River valley, Agony Grind and eastern Sterling Forest.

The A.T. now descends the mountain on switchbacks. You can hear the sound of traffic below, which means your car is not far away. At 6.4 miles (7.85 miles on the double loop), you'll reach the foot of Green Pond Mountain, where a wooden signpost marks the junction with Arden Road. Turn right onto Arden Road, but in 100 feet turn left and follow the A.T. across the meadow and back to the Elk Pen parking area and your car. 🥾

Chapter 14 Stockbridge Mountain and Lake Nawahunta

Rating:	**Easy to moderate**
Distance:	**5.2 miles**
Hiking Time:	**3 hours**
Attractions:	**Mountain top views, scenic lake, mine, rock cave shelter, overhanging perched boulder**
Lowest Elevation:	**715 feet**
Highest Elevation:	**1,300 feet**
Total Elevation Gain:	**990 feet**
Parking GPS Coordinates:	**41.29531, -74.05958**
Map:	**NY-NJ TC Northern Harriman-Bear Mountain Trails – Map #119**

Access: Take N.J. Route 17 north to the New York State Thruway and take the first exit, Exit 15A (Sloatsburg). Turn left at the bottom of the ramp onto N.Y. Route 17 north and continue through the village of Sloatsburg. Just beyond the village, turn right at the next traffic light, following the signs for Seven Lakes Drive and Harriman State Park. Follow Seven Lakes Drive for 12.4 miles to the Silvermine Picnic Area, on your right. Park in the west (right) end of the parking area, near the picnic area. On weekends during the summer, a parking fee is charged.

Description: Begin the hike by following the yellow-blazed Menomine Trail west on a paved gravel road which parallels a stream and leads through a picnic area. Just beyond a cable barrier, the trail turns right, crosses an abandoned paved road, and continues through a pine plantation. You will pass the family cemetery plot of James H. Lewis (1833-1907), a local farmer, and follow the Menomine Trail across Seven Lakes Drive. The trail continues along a woods road, the Nawahunta Fire Road, parallel to the shore of Lake Nawahunta.

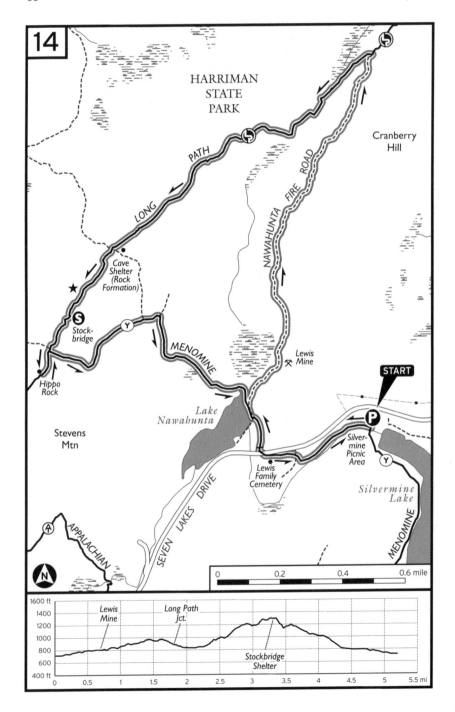

About 750 feet from Seven Lakes Drive, after passing a cellar hole on the left, the yellow-blazed Menomine Trail turns left, leaving the fire road. The Menomine Trail will be your return route, but for now, you should bear right and continue to follow the fire road. 0.15 mile after leaving the Menomine Trail, you will pass the Lewis Mine, which is easy to miss because the cut in the rock is angled away from the trail.

Monument for James H. Lewis

A small rock cairn on the right side of the fire road marks the location of the mine, which is about 50 feet off trail on the right. If you pass by the phragmites-filled swamp on your left, you have gone too far.

Lewis Mine

After taking a look at the mine, continue ahead along the Nawahunta Fire Road. The road climbs gradually for 0.9 mile through hardwoods and mountain laurel stands, passing many large boulders and a vernal pond. At 1.8 miles, after a brief descent, you'll reach a junction with the aqua-blazed Long Path. Make a sharp left here, leaving the Nawahunta Fire Road, and follow the Long Path southbound on a much rockier woods road. The Long Path descends into a wet area,

Lake Nawahunta

crossing Deep Hollow, then climbs steadily for 0.75 mile to the ridgeline of Stockbridge Mountain. In another 0.2 mile, you will reach the Stockbridge Cave Shelter, which is worth exploring. This shelter has a fireplace with a stone chimney and multiple hidden passageways through the rocks. You have now traveled 3.0 miles.

The Long Path continues to the right of the shelter, scrambling up some rocks and reaching the grassy summit of Stockbridge Mountain. The roof of the Stockbridge Shelter should be visible ahead, and to your right are bare rocks from which you can view the Arden House to the west (see Chapter 17 for more information on the Arden House). Continue past Stockbridge Shelter (built in 1928) and descend a ledge into a hardwood forest, reaching the end of the Menomine Trail, which is marked by a triple yellow blaze.

Stockbridge Cave Shelter

Stockbridge Shelter

Continue straight ahead on the Long Path for another 0.15 mile to the precariously perched overhanging boulder known as Hippo Rock. The rock is just off trail on your right. After exploring it, turn around and retrace your steps back to the Menomine Trail. You've now hiked 3.7 miles. Turn right at the triple yellow blaze and follow the yellow-blazed trail downhill on a rocky woods road. You will be following this trail for the remainder of the hike.

In 0.65 mile, the trail flattens out and passes through a pine plantation near Lake Nawahunta. Cross the outlet of Lake Nawahunta on stepping stones, then turn right, briefly following the eastern shore of the lake. Just ahead, you'll rejoin the Nawahunta Fire Road. The rest of the route back to the parking area will look familiar, since you covered it in reverse at the beginning of the hike. Cross Seven Lakes Drive and follow the yellow blazes 0.4 mile back to the parking area and your car.

Note: The Nawahunta Fire Road is smooth enough to trail run. If you run from the Silvermine Picnic Area to the northern end of the road (at Route 6) and back, you will have covered 4.4 miles. 🥾

Hippo Rock

Chapter 15 Silvermine Lake and Black Mountain

Rating:	**Moderate to strenuous**
Distance:	**5.0 miles**
Hiking Time:	**3 hours**
Attractions:	**Spectacular views of Silvermine Lake, the Hudson River and surrounding mountains, a stone shelter and a mine**
Lowest Elevation:	**665 feet**
Highest Elevation:	**1,200 feet**
Total Elevation Gain:	**1,125 feet**
Parking GPS Coordinates:	**41.29531, -74.05958**
Map:	**NY-NJ TC Northern Harriman-Bear Mountain Trails – Map #119**

Access: Take N.J. Route 17 north to the New York State Thruway and take the first exit, Exit 15A (Sloatsburg). Turn left at the bottom of the ramp onto N.Y. Route 17 north and continue through the village of Sloatsburg. Just beyond the village, turn right at the next traffic light, following the signs for Seven Lakes Drive and Harriman State Park. Follow Seven Lakes Drive for 12.4 miles to the Silvermine Picnic Area, on your right. On weekends during the summer, a parking fee is charged.

Description: Begin by walking toward the grassy ski slopes. Cross a stream on a brown-painted bridge and follow the yellow-blazed Menomine Trail, which turns left onto a dirt road, passing two park maintenance buildings on the left. Just before reaching Silvermine Lake, turn right, then bear left when you reach a brown-painted cinder block building. Here, the yellow blazes resume. Follow the trail into the woods on a rocky footpath, which soon begins to run along the shore of Silvermine Lake. At 0.45 mile, you will reach a good view of Black Mountain (across the lake) and be joined by a woods road coming up from the lake.

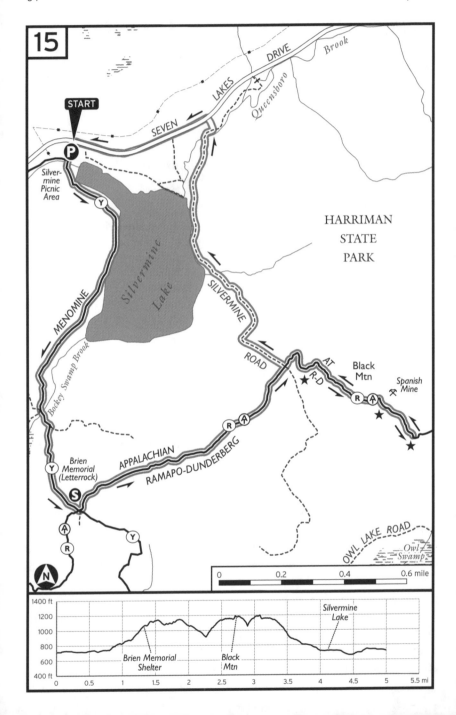

15

START

P

Silvermine Picnic Area

SEVEN LAKES DRIVE

Queensboro Brook

Silvermine Lake

MENOMINE

Buckey Swamp Brook

SILVERMINE ROAD

HARRIMAN STATE PARK

AT

R-D

Black Mtn

Spanish Mine

Brien Memorial (Letterrock)

APPALACHIAN

RAMAPO-DUNDERBERG

OWL LAKE ROAD

Owl Swamp

N

0   0.2   0.4   0.6 mile

1400 ft
1200
1000
800
600
400 ft

Brien Memorial Shelter

Black Mtn

Silvermine Lake

0   0.5   1   1.5   2   2.5   3   3.5   4   4.5   5   5.5 mi

Silvermine Lake

Beyond the end of the lake, the trail begins to climb along Bockey Swamp Brook, crossing several wet areas on rocks. Almost a mile into the hike, the yellow trail reaches another woods road. Turn left here (still following the yellow blazes) and cross a stream on a metal culvert. You will now begin a steady 0.35-mile climb to the William Brien Memorial Shelter, reached at 1.35 miles. William Brien was the first president of the New York Ramblers and, when he died in 1954, he bequeathed $4,000 for the construction of a shelter in Harriman State Park. In 1957, a shelter was built in his memory at Island Pond, but this shelter was removed in 1973 due to vandalism, and the Letterrock Shelter, built in 1933, was renamed the William Brien Memorial Shelter. Just beyond the shelter, you will intersect the co-aligned Appalachian and Ramapo-Dunderberg Trails (A.T./R-D). The A.T.

William Brien Memorial Shelter

is blazed white, while the R-D has a red dot on a white background.

Turn left on the A.T./R-D, scrambling up rocks. The trail heads northeast, with some minor ups and downs, and then descends steadily. At the base of the descent, 2.25 miles from the start, the trail crosses the Silvermine Road –

Silvermine Road

an unmarked but well-defined "stone road," with distinctive stone embankments, built in 1934 by workers of the Temporary Emergency Relief Administration. You will come back to this location later on in the hike.

For now, continue ahead on the A.T./R-D, crossing a small stream, and immediately beginning a steep ascent of Black Mountain. Soon, you will reach a ledge with impressive views of Silvermine Lake. After a few more short climbs, you will pass just below the summit. Just beyond, at the height of land on the trail, a clearing on the left leads to an exploratory pit and a deep, flooded hole known as the Spanish Mine or the Spanish Silver Mine. Ironically, no silver was ever found here.

View of Silvermine Lake from A.T./R-D

East-facing view from the summit of Black Mountain

Continue on the A.T./R-D for another 0.2 mile, enjoying excellent views of the Hudson River to the southeast, with West Mountain to the east and Bear Mountain to the northeast. To the south, you can see Owl Swamp (directly below) and the AT&T microwave relay towers on Jackie Jones Mountain in the distance. Where the trail turns left and begins a steep descent, turn around and retrace your steps, heading west across the summit ridge and then back down Black Mountain. At the base of the descent, after crossing the stream, turn right onto Silvermine Road – the unmarked "stone road" you crossed earlier. You have now traveled 3.65 miles.

The road heads downhill at a gentle pitch. There a few rocky sections, but most of the road is smooth enough to run. After about half a mile, you will cross an inlet and reach the northeastern shore of Silvermine Lake. In another quarter mile, the road turns away from the lake and descends along a stream, then crosses the stream on a wide wooden bridge. Just beyond, as the road curves to the right, you'll notice the embankment of Seven Lakes Drive on the left. When the road again curves to the right, turn left onto an unmarked trail and follow it a short distance up to Seven Lakes Drive. Turn left and follow the shoulder of the Drive for about 0.4 mile to the Silvermine Picnic Area, where the hike began. ⚑

Chapter 16   Appalachian Trail-Long Path Loop

Rating:	**Moderate to strenuous**
Distance:	**5.5 miles**
Hiking Time:	**3.5 to 4 hours**
Attractions:	**Diverse scenery, a large mine, wetlands, shelters, winter views of Lake Tiorati**
Lowest Elevation:	**995 feet**
Highest Elevation:	**1,378 feet**
Total Elevation Gain:	**1,280 feet**
Parking GPS Coordinates:	**41.27510, -74.08925**
Map:	**NY-NJ TC Northern Harriman-Bear Mountain Trails – Map #119**

Access: Take N.J. Route 17 north to the New York State Thruway and take the first exit, Exit 15A (Sloatsburg). Turn left at the bottom of the ramp onto N.Y. Route 17 north and continue through the village of Sloatsburg. Just beyond the village, turn right at the next traffic light, following the signs for Seven Lakes Drive and Harriman State Park. Follow Seven Lakes Drive for 10.3 miles to Tiorati Circle (the second circle). Go three-quarters of the way around the circle and proceed west on Arden Valley Road. Almost immediately, turn left into the Tiorati parking area and park just beyond the first dumpster on the right. A parking fee may be charged during the summer (Memorial Day weekend through Labor Day).

Description: Although this hike is only 5.5 miles long, it may feel a bit longer due to the six climbs it makes along the way.

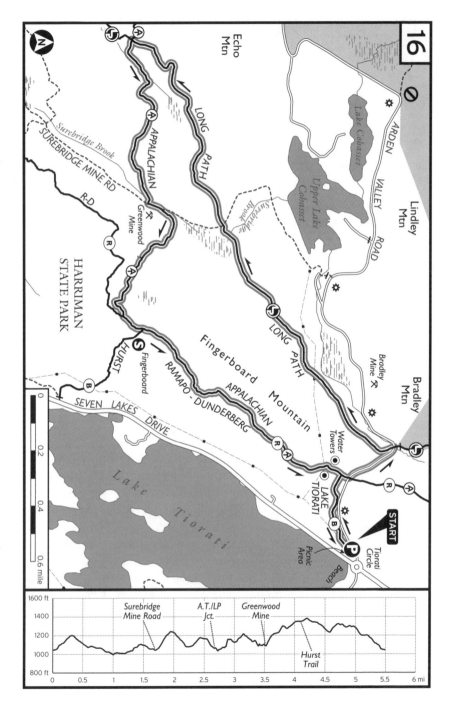

Find the start of the Lake Tiorati Trail, marked by a triple blue blaze, and follow the trail for 0.3 mile up to the crest of Fingerboard Mountain, paralleling the paved Arden Valley Road. At the top, turn right onto a gravel road, then turn left onto Arden Valley Road and proceed downhill for 0.2 mile. At a bend in the road at the bottom of the hill, turn left onto the aqua-blazed Long Path, which follows a rocky footpath through a wet area. After a gradual descent, you'll pass a cliff on the left in an area of hemlocks and mountain laurel.

Just beyond, the Long Path turns left, crosses over three pipes, and passes through dense mountain laurel thickets. It next crosses three small streams. After crossing a fourth stream, the trail begins a gradual climb, joining an old woods road and crossing another stream along the way. After reaching the height of land (marked by three boulders on the right), the Long Path begins to descend. At the base of the descent, it passes to the right of a phragmites-filled wetland.

A short distance beyond, the Long Path crosses Surebridge Brook on rocks just above a breached dam. It passes a flooded mine pit on the left and crosses the unmarked Surebridge Mine Road, 1.7 miles from the start. The trail now proceeds uphill, passing to the left of a corrugated-metal trail shelter (built in 1937 for use by the girls' camps on Upper Lake Cohasset). It then climbs more steeply to an open rock ledge, with limited views over Lindley and Bradley Mountains and (when there are no leaves on the trees) Upper Lake Cohasset.

A hiker approaching the phragmites-filled wetland

Upper Lake Cohasset camp shelter

After continuing to the crest of the rise, the trail descends into a scenic hollow, passing to the right of another phragmites-filled wetland. It then climbs through hemlocks to a secondary summit of Echo Mountain (1,180 feet), from where it makes a winding descent into a hemlock-filled hollow. Here, at 2.7 miles, it reaches a junction with the white-blazed Appalachian Trail (A.T.). This intersection of two major long distance trails is marked by a wooden signpost which gives detailed mileage information in all directions.

Turn left here, following the white-blazed A.T. downhill to a stream. The A.T. bears left and begins to parallel the stream. It crosses the stream, again parallels it on the other side, then turns right and begins to climb Surebridge Mountain. At first, the trail climbs steeply over rocks and exposed tree roots. At the top of the steep climb, it bears left and descends through a

Four-tiered mileage signpost

valley. It then bears right and climbs to the height of land on the crest of Surebridge Mountain.

The A.T. now descends gradually. Near the base of the descent, it passes by a small wetland. A short distance beyond, it descends to Surebridge Brook, which it crosses on rocks. On the other side of the brook, the A.T. turns left onto the unmarked Surebridge Mine Road. In a short distance, you'll reach the Greenwood Mine,

Greenwood Mine

marked by a 100-foot-long flooded mine pit on your right and a huge pile of tailings on the left. The dark, almost bluish color of the iron ore found here indicates that it was probably of very high quality. Note the drill marks in the rocks on the sides of the mine. You'll also see a rusted pipe and stone foundations at the northern end of the mine.

After descending a short distance on Surebridge Mine Road (and passing a smaller mine pit on the right),

Along the ridge of Fingerboard Mountain

the A.T. turns right at 3.55 miles and begins a steep climb on an eroded trail, with many exposed tree routes. The grade soon moderates. After climbing through dense mountain laurel thickets, the trail bears right and levels off. It climbs steeply over rock ledges, passes through more dense mountain laurel thickets, then ascends on a rocky switchback to the bare summit ridge of Fingerboard Mountain.

At 4.05 miles, at the crest of the ridge, the A.T. joins the Ramapo-Dunderberg (R-D) Trail, which comes in from the right. Turn left and follow the co-aligned A.T. and R-D along the ridge. Much of the trail is on bare rock – a welcome contrast from the terrain you've past through until now. Soon, you'll pass the trailhead of the blue-blazed Hurst Trail on the right. This trail leads downhill to the stone Fingerboard Shelter, built in 1928.

The joint A.T./R-D now passes just to the east of Fingerboard Mountain's 1,378-foot summit. It soon descends to a col. As you climb back up to the ridge, you'll pass an interesting rock formation on the left. At the height of land, there is an interesting balanced rock just to the left of the trail. Continue following the ridgeline to the northeast, with Lake Tiorati often visible through the trees on the right if the leaves are down.

Balanced rock along the A.T./R-D

Water tanks

After descending more steeply, the A.T./R-D passes between two water tanks. The concrete water tank on the right was built in 1927 and was replaced in 2006 by the larger tank on the left, which is surrounded by a chain-link fence. A short distance beyond, you'll reach the western end of the blue-blazed Lake Tiorati Trail, which begins on the right. Turn right and follow the Lake Tiorati Trail for 0.3 mile downhill, retracing your steps to the parking lot where the hike began. 🚶

Chapter 17　Goshen Mountain

Rating:	**Moderate**
Distance:	**6.95 miles**
Hiking Time:	**3.5 to 4 hours**
Attractions:	**Winter views from Goshen and Stevens Mountains**
Lowest Elevation:	**840 feet**
Highest Elevation:	**1,300 feet**
Total Elevation Gain:	**1,425 feet**
Parking GPS Coordinates:	**41.27510, -74.08925**
Map:	**NY-NJ TC Northern Harriman-Bear Mountain Trails – Map #119**

Access: Take N.J. Route 17 north to the New York State Thruway and take the first exit, Exit 15A (Sloatsburg). Turn left at the bottom of the ramp onto N.Y. Route 17 north, and continue through the village of Sloatsburg. Just beyond the village, turn right at the next traffic light, following the signs for Seven Lakes Drive and Harriman State Park. Follow Seven Lakes Drive for 10.3 miles to Tiorati Circle (the second circle). Go three-quarters of the way around the circle and proceed west on Arden Valley Road. Almost immediately, turn left into the Tiorati parking area and park just beyond the first dumpster on the right. A parking fee may be charged during the summer (Memorial Day weekend through Labor Day).

Description: The views will be much better if you take this hike between mid-November and late March, when the leaves are down.

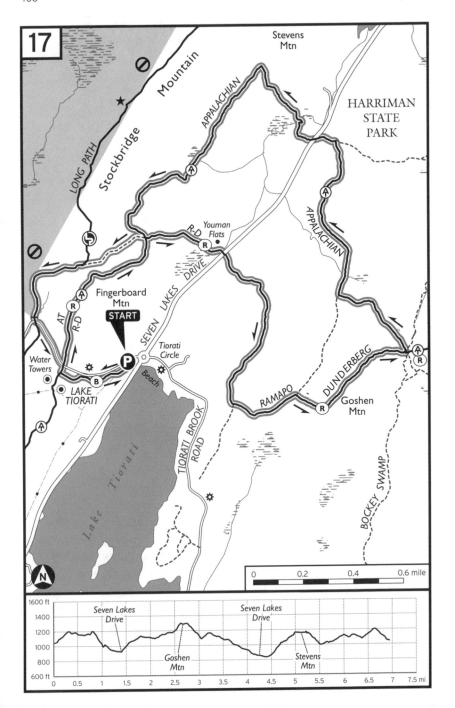

DAN BALOGH

Lake Tiorati

Find the start of the Lake Tiorati Trail, marked by a triple blue blaze just south of the first dumpster on the west side of the parking area. Follow it up to the crest of Fingerboard Mountain, paralleling Arden Valley Road. For part of the way, the trail follows an older route of Arden Valley Road. In 0.3 mile, the Lake Tiorati Trail ends at a junction with the white-blazed Appalachian Trail (A.T.) and the red-dot-on-white-blazed Ramapo-Dunderberg (R-D) Trail. Turn right here, following the co-aligned A.T. and R-D across Arden Valley Road and through a mixed hardwood forest and mountain laurel thicket. After a steady, rather steep descent, the trail crosses a small stream and climbs to a wide woods road (the original Arden Valley Road) at 1.05 miles. Here, the two trails diverge.

To the left, the woods road will be your return route, but for now, you should turn right onto the road and head downhill, following the red-dot-on-white blazes of the R-D Trail. After crossing a wooden bridge over a stream, the trail turns right at a chain-link fence by the Youmans Flats maintenance area, then turns right again, joining the road leading into the maintenance area. It passes through a small pine grove and soon reaches Seven Lakes Drive.

Wooden footbridge over a stream on the A.T.

Continue to follow the R-D Trail as it crosses the road and begins a steady climb. After the trail levels off, you'll pass winter views of Lake Tiorati to the right. The R-D Trail then turns left and climbs a little. At 2.45 miles, it turns right and begins to climb more steeply. In 0.2 mile, you'll reach the ridge of Goshen Mountain, which is covered with blueberry bushes and has relatively few trees. As you head northeast along the ridgeline, you can see the Hudson River through the trees to your right. To the left, there are wintertime views of Stockbridge Mountain and the Arden House on Mount Aramah. Edward Harriman built this mansion between 1906 and 1909, but sadly, he died just weeks after its completion.

After reaching the 1,320-foot summit, the trail descends moderately on a grassy footpath. Ahead, through the trees, you may spot Silvermine Lake, as well as Bear Mountain and the Perkins Memorial Tower (which is about five miles away to the northeast). At 3.05 miles, at the base of the descent, you will reach the intersection of the R-D Trail, the A.T. and the unmarked Bockey Swamp Trail. The R-D Trail turns right here, but you should turn left, following the white-blazed A.T.

The A.T. descends for about a mile along a woods road, then turns left onto another woods road, which joins from the right. At 4.25 miles, the A.T. crosses Seven Lakes Drive diagonally to the left and enters a rocky, wet area. After crossing three small streams on rocks and a wider stream on a wooden bridge, the A.T. begins to climb Stevens Mountain. At first the climb is rather steep, but the grade moderates soon after the trail turns left and begins to follow the ridgeline.

An interesting boulder along the A.T.

Near the top of the ridge, the A.T. levels off and crosses the outlet of a wetland to the right. A short distance beyond, at 5.15 miles, you'll come to a rock outcrop, with winter views through the trees of Lake Tiorati and Fingerboard Mountain. This is a good spot to take a break.

DAN BALOGH

Pine trees along the A.T. on Stevens Mountain

South-facing view over Fingerboard Mountain from the ridge of Stevens Mountain

The A.T. now bears right and descends on a footpath that soon widens to a woods road. After crossing a stream, the trail climbs a little on a footpath, reaching a grassy woods road at 5.7 miles. You were at this spot earlier in the hike. This time, you should turn right, following the grassy woods road uphill. Although the road is not blazed, its route is obvious and easily followed. In 0.3 mile, at a cairn at the crest of the rise, the aqua-blazed Long Path joins from the right. Continue following the woods road as it descends gently for 0.4 mile to Arden Valley Road. Turn left on the paved Arden Valley Road (leaving the Long Path) and walk along the road for 0.2 mile to the top of the hill, where the white-blazed A.T. and the red-dot-on-white-blazed R-D Trail cross the road. Turn right onto the A.T./R-D and, in 200 feet, turn left onto the blue-blazed Lake Tiorati Trail. Follow this trail downhill for 0.3 mile to the parking lot where the hike began. 🚶

Chapter 18 Pine Swamp Mountain

Shorter Hike

Rating:	**Easy to moderate**
Distance:	**3.7 miles**
Hiking Time:	**2.25 hours**
Attractions:	**Remnants of several large iron mines**
Lowest Elevation:	**890 feet**
Highest Elevation:	**1,255 feet**
Total Elevation Gain:	**725 feet**

Longer Hike

Rating:	**Strenuous**
Distance:	**5.95 miles**
Hiking Time:	**4.5 hours**
Attractions:	**Remnants of several large iron mines**
Lowest Elevation:	**890 feet**
Highest Elevation:	**1,367 feet**
Total Elevation Gain:	**1,305 feet**

Parking GPS Coordinates:	**41.24202, -74.10229**
Map:	**NY-NJ TC Northern Harriman-Bear Mountain Trails – Map #119**

Access: Take N.J. Route 17 north to the New York State Thruway and take the first exit, Exit 15A (Sloatsburg). Turn left at the bottom of the ramp onto N.Y. Route 17 north, and continue through the village of Sloatsburg. Just beyond the village, turn right at the next traffic light, following the signs for Seven Lakes Drive and Harriman State Park. Follow Seven Lakes Drive for 7.1 miles and proceed straight across Kanawauke Circle. Continue following Seven Lakes Drive for another 0.7 mile to the parking lot for Lake Skannatati, on the left side of the road.

Caution: Due to a difficult crossing of Surebridge Brook, you may wish to avoid the longer hike when water levels are high (such as after heavy rains).

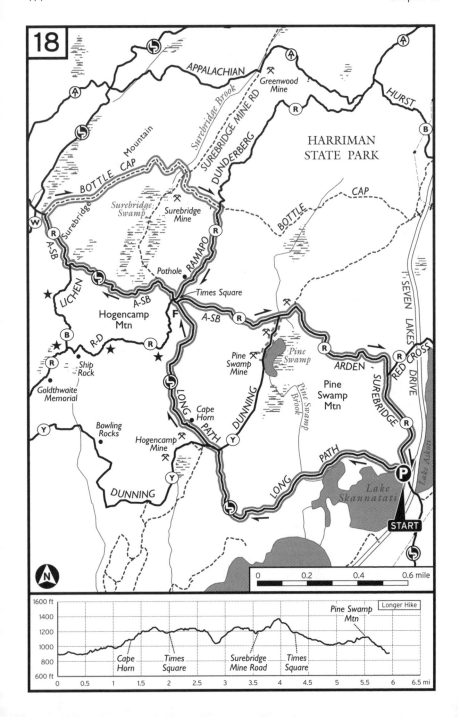

High rock ledge along the Long Path

Description: From the kiosk at the northwest corner of the parking lot, bear left and follow the aqua blazes of the Long Path along the north shore of Lake Skannatati on a heavily used, wide and rocky footpath. After crossing Pine Swamp Brook on rocks, the trail veers away from the lake and passes a high rock ledge to the right. If you have time, you may wish to explore the ledge and try to find a tiny hidden hollow on top of its northern end. Continuing on the Long Path, you will pass through dense mountain laurel thickets and cross one more stream before climbing to a junction at 1.25 miles with the yellow-blazed Dunning Trail (blazed in 1933 by Dr. James M. Dunning of the Appalachian Mountain Club).

Bear left and follow the co-aligned Long Path and Dunning Trail for about 200 feet, then bear right at the fork, continuing uphill on the Long Path. Just before reaching a large boulder and a rock formation known as Cape Horn, you'll pass an interesting mine shaft, directly below you on your left. If you wish to get a better look at the mine shaft, carefully descend the steep slope to reach the entrance. For safety's sake, keep well to the left of the open mine cut as you

Cape Horn

descend. This mine is part of the Hogencamp Mine complex, which was active from 1870 to 1885.

The Long Path continues to climb, entering the site of a 2001 forest fire which burned most of the immature trees. The trail passes glacial erratics and the remains of an old foundation (part of the mining operation) before descending through young hemlocks, mountain laurel and fallen trees. At 2.0 miles, you will reach an intersection with the inverted-red-triangle-on-white-blazed Arden-Surebridge (A-SB) Trail. Just beyond, you'll come to "Times Square" – marked by a large boulder and a fireplace. "Times Square" gets its name because it is where three trails come together – the A-SB Trail, the Long Path and the red-dot-on-white-blazed Ramapo-Dunderberg Trail.

Shorter hike: Retrace your steps to the junction of the A-SB Trail with the Long Path and bear left, now following only the inverted-red-triangle-on-white blazes of the A-SB Trail. Do not follow the red-dot-on-white blazes of the R-D Trail or the aqua blazes of the Long Path. Now skip ahead to the section of this chapter marked "Return Trip."

Longer hike: Continue following the co-aligned inverted-red-triangle-on-white-blazed A-SB Trail and aqua-blazed Long Path, which climbs over rocks and through mountain laurel thickets. At 2.6 miles, the blue-"L"-on-white-blazed Lichen Trail begins on the left, but you should continue to follow the A-SB Trail/

Long Path. After skirting a small wetland, you'll begin to descend. Near the bottom, at 2.85 miles, you'll cross a small stream and reach a T-intersection. Here, the A-SB/Long Path turns left, but you should turn right onto the Bottle Cap Trail, which begins here (the start of this trail is marked by three bottle caps nailed to a tree). Although not maintained by the Trail Conference, the Bottle Cap Trail is shown on Map #119. (If you reach a junction with the White Bar Trail on your left, you have gone about 300 feet too far.)

The Bottle Cap Trail heads uphill on a wide path for 350 feet, then turns right onto a narrower path and climbs Surebridge Mountain, passing through a hemlock forest. The trail follows the ridge for 0.15 mile and then makes several steep descents before crossing Surebridge Brook and reaching Surebridge Mine Road (marked by a cairn) at 3.6 miles. (Note: The crossing of Surebridge Brook can be difficult if water levels are high. You may need to explore upstream or downstream to find a suitable place to cross.) If you wish to take a short side trip, a flooded shaft of the Surebridge Mine can be found 0.1 mile south of this intersection on the left side of Surebridge Mine Road.

A hiker at Times Square

After crossing Surebridge Mine Road, the Bottle Cap Trail climbs a hill and passes a stone structure on the right and mine tailings and a water-filled pit on the left. At 3.8 miles, you'll reach an intersection with the red-dot-on-white-blazed Ramapo-Dunderberg (R-D) Trail.

Turn right onto the R-D Trail, and continue climbing for 0.2 mile through a hemlock grove. After reaching the 1,367-foot summit, you'll descend gradually through white pines, chestnut oaks and mountain laurel, then bear right and follow the trail down a rocky ledge. There is a pothole in the ledge, just to the right of the trail. In another 0.1 mile, you'll reach Times Square, which you passed earlier in your hike. You have now hiked 4.3 miles. Turn left here and, almost immediately, turn left again, now following only the inverted-red-triangle-on-white blazes of the Arden-Surebridge (A-SB) Trail.

Return Trip: The A-SB Trail descends gently along the route of an old mining road (an extension of what is known today as Surebridge Mine Road). This section of trail was devastated by Hurricane Sandy in October 2012, and Trail Conference volunteers spent many hours removing the blowdowns with their chainsaws. In half a mile, just after passing the remnants of an old foundation on your left, you'll reach the northern end of the Dunning Trail at a beautiful cascade. For a worthwhile side trip, turn right on the Dunning Trail and walk downhill. In 0.15 mile, as you pass the interesting Pine Swamp on the left, you'll notice a large

Entrance to the shaft of the Pine Swamp Mine

DAN BALOGH

Opening of the Pine Swamp Mine along the A-SB Trail

pile of mine tailings on your right. Climb the tailings pile on an unmarked path, then bear left at the top to reach a 25-foot-deep cut in the rock. At the end of the rock cut, an eerie-looking mine shaft has been tunneled into the mountain. Your footsteps may echo as you enter the tunnel! The rock cut and mine shaft were part of the Pine Swamp Mine, another mining venture in the area, which was opened about 1830 and worked intermittently until 1880. Return as you came, and turn right onto the A-SB Trail. This side trip will add about 0.4 mile and 25 minutes to your hike.

Follow the A-SB Trail as it crosses the stream on rocks. Just beyond, you'll notice several rectangular cuts in the rock, mine tailings and water-filled pits on the left. These are also remnants of the Pine Swamp Mine. Soon, the A-SB Trail bears right, leaving the old mine road, and descends past stone foundations – remnants of the village associated with the Pine Swamp Mine – and the northeastern end of Pine Swamp.

After climbing gradually, the A-SB levels off along a shoulder of Pine Swamp Mountain and soon reaches a junction with the Red Cross Trail, which begins on the left. Continue along the A-SB Trail, which now descends gradually, with views to the left of Lake Askoti when the leaves are down. At the base of the descent, you'll reach the parking lot at Lake Skannatati and your car. 🥾

Chapter 19 Hasenclever Mine

Shorter Hike

Rating:	**Easy to moderate**
Distance:	**5.95 miles**
Hiking Time:	**3.5 hours**
Attractions:	**Interesting rock formations, Hasenclever Mine, a Civil War-era cemetery, and large laurel groves (best viewed while in-bloom in the spring)**
Lowest Elevation:	**890 feet**
Highest Elevation:	**1,180 feet**
Total Elevation Gain:	**1,065 feet**

Longer Hike

Rating:	**Moderate**
Distance:	**8.4 miles**
Hiking Time:	**5.5 hours**
Attractions:	**Interesting rock formations, cascades, Hasenclever Mine, a Civil War-era cemetery, and large laurel groves (best viewed while in-bloom in the spring)**
Lowest Elevation:	**705 feet**
Highest Elevation:	**1,180 feet**
Total Elevation Gain:	**1,455 feet**
Parking GPS Coordinates:	**41.24202, -74.10229**
Map:	**NY-NJ TC Northern Harriman-Bear Mountain Trails – Map #119**

Access: Take N.J. Route 17 north to the New York State Thruway and take the first exit, Exit 15A (Sloatsburg). Turn left at the bottom of the ramp onto N.Y. Route 17 north, and continue through the village of Sloatsburg. Just beyond the village, turn right at the next traffic light, following the signs for Seven Lakes Drive and Harriman State Park. Follow Seven Lakes Drive for 7.1 miles and

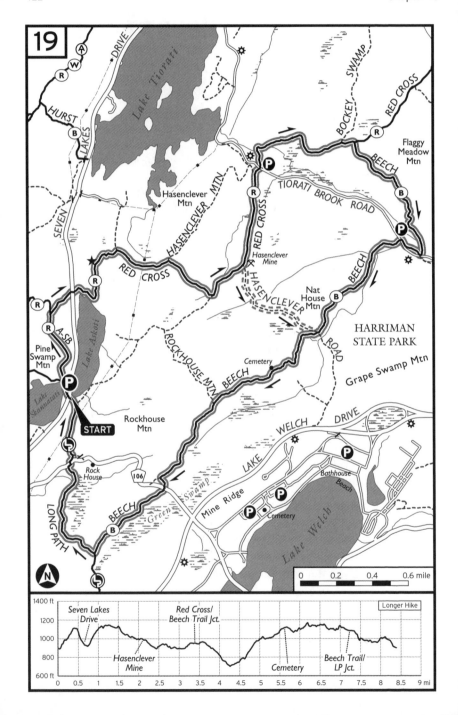

proceed straight across Kanawauke Circle. Continue following Seven Lakes Drive for another 0.7 mile to the parking area for Lake Skannatati, on the left side of the road.

Description: From a kiosk at the northwest corner of the parking area, follow the inverted-red-triangle-on-white-blazed Arden-Surebridge (A-SB) Trail, which bears right, climbs stone steps, and begins to climb Pine Swamp Mountain on a moderate grade through a mixed hardwood forest. As the trail bends to the left, there are seasonal views of Lake Askoti, below to the right. Just beyond the crest of the rise, you'll notice the start of the Red Cross Trail on the right, marked by triple blazes of a red cross on a

Stone steps on the A-SB Trail

white background. Turn right and follow the Red Cross Trail, which descends steadily to Seven Lakes Drive, crossing it 0.65 mile from the start.

On the other side of the paved road, the trail descends slightly, turns right over a short rise (a rock outcrop on the right offers a panoramic view of Lake Askoti), and descends again to cross the inlet stream of Lake Askoti. The trail now begins a steady climb through dense mountain laurel, with views over the lake through the trees to the right. Soon, the trail bends sharply left and continues its gradual climb of an arm of Hasenclever Mountain. Near the top of the ascent, a rock outcrop to the left offers views of Pine Swamp Mountain and the bare rocks of Hogencamp Mountain to the southwest.

The trail crosses an interesting hollow, climbs past an unmarked trail that begins on the left (the junction is marked by a cairn), levels off

Lake Askoti from rock outcrop along the Red Cross Trail

Hasenclever Mine

and crosses a gravel road under a power line. It turns right at a T-intersection, where the unmarked Hasenclever Mountain Trail goes left. Continue on the Red Cross Trail, which descends gradually on a woods road and crosses a stream on a wooden bridge. A short distance beyond, at 1.85 miles, the trail turns left onto another woods road and descends for a quarter mile to the Hasenclever Mine complex. There are several pits on the left and a flooded mine shaft on the right, just beyond the junction with Hasenclever Road, which comes in from the right. The Hasenclever Mine was first opened in 1760 by Baron Peter Hasenclever, who dammed the Cedar Ponds to create the present-day Lake Tiorati.

Shorter hike: Turn right on the unmarked Hasenclever Road, which you will follow for two-thirds of a mile. The road descends gradually, crosses a small brook on a concrete bridge (a reminder that, until 1910, this was a county road), and begins a gradual climb up Nat House Mountain. Next, the road descends for about 0.1 mile before reaching the blue-blazed Beech Trail. Turn right on the Beech Trail and skip ahead to the section of this chapter marked "Return Trip." You have now traveled 2.75 miles.

Longer hike: Proceed ahead on the Red Cross Trail, which follows a woods road for another half mile, forks right off the woods road (easy to miss), continues through a wet section and crosses the paved Tiorati Brook Road. The trail turns left, goes across a ballfield, to cross the beautiful cascading Tiorati Brook on rocks, and turns right to briefly parallel the brook. After crossing a tributary stream, the trail goes past a swampy area and up a small hill. Here you will cross the unmarked Bockey Swamp Trail (marked by a cairn) and, in another 0.1 mile, reach a junction with the blue-blazed Beech Trail (marked by a large cairn). You have now hiked 3.4 miles.

First blazed in 1972, the Beech Trail was the first trail to use offset blazes to designate turn directions. This blazing convention was invented by Bob Fuller, a member of the Trail Conference, and has now been adopted for all trails by the Trail Conference and many other organizations.

Turn right on the Beech Trail and follow it for 0.9 mile as it descends to Tiorati Brook Road. Continue to follow the blue blazes as the trail turns right to cross Tiorati Brook on the road bridge and then bears right and follows a narrow path along the brook. The Beech Trail rejoins the road briefly to cross a tributary of Tiorati Brook, follows along the road for about 200 feet, then crosses the road and continues uphill, parallel to the tributary stream, on an eroded woods road. In 0.3 mile, you'll cross a small wooden bridge and begin climbing more steeply. Look to your left for a short unmarked path to Arthur's Falls, a beautiful cascade, which makes a nice lunch spot for a small group. After 0.75 mile of climbing up Nat House Mountain, continue on the Beech Trail as it crosses the unmarked Hasenclever Road. You have now traveled 5.2 miles.

Return Trip: The trail climbs gradually as it heads south through mountain laurels and hardwoods, crossing a stream on rocks. In a third of a mile, you'll climb a short, rather steep pitch and reach the remains of an old farm, with a number of stone walls. Soon, you will pass a small cemetery on the right that dates back to the Civil War. In another 0.4 mile, the unmarked Rockhouse Mountain Trail begins on your right (this junction is marked by a cairn). A short distance beyond, as the trail passes below the summit of Rockhouse Mountain, you'll notice a balanced glacial erratic on a rock ledge to the left.

Balanced glacial erratic along the Beech Trail

Cemetery on the Beech Trail

The trail now descends gradually and turns left off the woods road (easy to miss) before crossing the paved Route 106 (Kanawauke Road). Continue through laurels, passing jumbled boulders and overhanging rocks on the right and a pretty, evergreen-lined swamp on the left. In 0.6 mile (from Route 106), you'll pass a stone foundation on the right and reach the end of the Beech Trail. Turn right here, following the aqua-colored blazes of the Long Path through the laurel, and descend to a phragmites-filled wetland on the right. After crossing its outlet on a bed of rocks and passing a stand of pine trees, you'll come to Route 106. Follow the Long Path, which turns right and continues along the road for about 150 feet, then turns left and climbs to a woods road.

The Long Path turns left onto the woods road, crosses under a power line and descends to Seven Lakes Drive. Turn right and follow Seven Lakes Drive, crossing a bridge over the outlet of Lake Askoti, then turn left, cross the road, and follow the Long Path downhill to the parking lot and your car. 🚶

Chapter 20

Long Mountain and Turkey Hill Lake

Rating:	**Easy to moderate**
Distance:	**5.1 miles (6.0 miles with optional side hike)**
Hiking Time:	**3.5 hours (4 hours with optional side hike)**
Attractions:	**Panoramic views from Torrey Memorial, scenic lakes and brooks**
Lowest Elevation:	**500 feet (455 feet with optional side hike)**
Highest Elevation:	**1,155 feet**
Total Elevation Gain:	**1,185 feet (1,300 feet with optional side hike)**
Parking GPS Coordinates:	**41.31638, -74.05053**
Map:	**NY-NJ TC Northern Harriman Bear Mountain Trails – Map #119**

Access: Take the Palisades Interstate Parkway north to Exit 18 (Central Valley / Seven Lakes Drive) and proceed ahead to the Long Mountain Circle. Take the second exit off the circle (halfway around) onto Route 6, and continue for 1.2 miles to a sign on the right side of the road for "Long Path/Raymond H. Torrey Memorial." Turn right and continue for 0.2 mile to a kiosk on the right.

Description: From the kiosk, head north into the woods on the aqua-blazed Long Path, following a woods road which soon becomes rather rocky and descends gently. At the base of the descent, the red-square-on-white-blazed Popolopen Gorge Trail begins on the right, but you should continue ahead on the Long Path, which bears slightly to the left and begins to climb, still following the woods road.

The trail climbs moderately at first, then bears right and climbs more steeply over rock slabs and steps. About 0.6 mile from the start, the trail reaches the open 1,155-foot summit of Long Mountain, which affords panoramic east-facing views

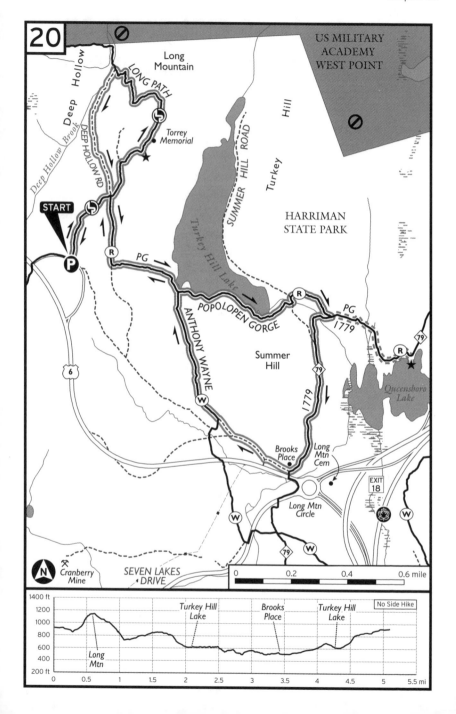

Turkey Hill Lake from Long Mountain

of Turkey Hill and Turkey Hill Lake. Behind Turkey Hill, one can see the bald-topped Popolopen Torne and Bear Mountain (the Perkins Memorial Tower is at its summit), with West Mountain to their right. A memorial to Raymond H. Torrey is carved in the bedrock underfoot. In addition to leading the New York-New Jersey Trail Conference, Torrey contributed greatly to the development of both the Long Path and the Appalachian Trail. It was Torrey who scouted this trail section in 1922.

After taking in the magnificent view, continue ahead on the Long Path. From the northern end of the summit ridge, there is a broad view to the north over the hills in the West Point Military Reservation. The trail now descends over open rock slabs. In another 0.2 mile, it turns left and continues to descend. The former Fingerboard-Storm King Trail, which extended north from Fingerboard Mountain to Storm King Mountain (crossing West Point property on the way), once headed north here. Pay close attention to the trail markers as the trail descends the mountain on switchbacks. Before you reach Deep Hollow Brook at the base of the descent, you'll pass the remains of the former Deep Hollow Shelter on the right. Just beyond, leave the Long Path and turn left onto an unmarked woods road. This "stone road," known as the Deep Hollow Road, was constructed by the Civilian Conservation Corps in 1934. The CCC workers laid a base of broken stone, but never completed the road by overlaying it with a layer of gravel.

The stone road parallels the brook for a short distance. It then bears left, away from the brook, and begins to climb, with Long Mountain on the left. In about half a mile, you'll reach the intersection of the Long Path and the Popolopen Gorge Trail that you passed earlier. Continue ahead, now following the red-square-on-white blazes of the Popolopen Gorge Trail, which proceeds through a beautiful valley and then begins a gentle descent.

In a quarter mile, the Popolopen Gorge Trail turns left, leaving the road, and descends more steeply, reaching Turkey Hill Lake at 2.1 miles. The trail crosses a grassy area and passes the start of the Anthony Wayne Trail on your right (this will be your return route). Turn left and continue to follow the Popolopen Gorge Trail, which runs parallel to the shore of the lake, with views over the lake. Long Mountain is visible on the left and Turkey Hill on the right. As you proceed east along the lakeshore, you'll come to a superb view of Bear Mountain. The trail swings

around the southern end of the dam and descends past a massive boulder. It turns left onto a woods road (Summer Hill Road), crosses the outlet of Turkey Hill Lake, and immediately turns right at a cairn onto a footpath, which climbs over a knoll.

At 2.85 miles, the Popolopen Gorge Trail reaches an intersection (marked by a cairn) with the 1779 Trail (blazed with a blue "1779" on a white background). At this point, you may either make a sharp right onto the 1779 Trail or take the following side trip which will add 0.9 mile to your hike.

Bear Mountain from Long Mountain

Torrey Memorial on Long Mountain

Side trip: Continue straight on the co-aligned Popolopen Gorge and 1779 Trails. After 0.45 mile of level walking, you will reach Queensboro Lake. At a double cairn on the right, turn right and walk out onto a peninsula that juts into the lake, with many open ledges that are good spots for a lunch break. Return as you came and, at the cairn at the trail junction, bear left onto the 1779 Trail.

The 1779 Trail descends to cross a brook on a wooden bridge (built in 2014 by the West Hudson and Long Distance Trails Crews of the Trail Conference) and heads uphill. In another 0.1 mile, the trail bears left onto Summer Hill Road. If the leaves are down, you will soon see Queensboro Lake on your left, with Bear Mountain in the background. In another half mile, after a slight climb, you'll reach the Brooks Place maintenance yard. Bear right and follow the gravel road (old Route 6) through the yard, passing to the right of a huge gravel pile. A short distance beyond, the 1779 Trail turns left to cross Route 6, but you should continue straight ahead on the older road (now paved), bearing right at the next intersection. In a quarter mile, you'll come to a sand-and-salt storage dome. Turn right, walk counter-clockwise around the back of the dome, and turn right onto an unmarked woods road. Follow the road for 200 feet to an intersection with the white-blazed Anthony Wayne Trail, then turn right and begin to follow the Anthony Wayne Trail.

Turkey Hill Lake

Follow the Anthony Wayne Trail along a grassy woods road which climbs over a knoll to its northern terminus at a junction with the red-square-on-white-blazed Popolopen Gorge Trail at the southwest corner of Turkey Hill Lake (you were at this intersection earlier). Not counting the side trip, you have now hiked for 4.25 miles. You might want to walk to the lakeshore and savor the views over the lake. When you're ready to continue, head west on the Popolopen Gorge Trail and follow it uphill for 0.3 mile. Here, the Popolopen Gorge Trail turns right on a woods road and ends at the aqua-blazed Long Path. Turn left on the Long Path and follow it back to your car. 🚶

Chapter 21 Pingyp Mountain

Rating:	**Strenuous**
Distance:	**7.1 miles**
Hiking Time:	**4 hours**
Attractions:	**Challenging and spectacular climbs, streams, wetlands, remote areas**
Lowest Elevation:	**400 feet**
Highest Elevation:	**1,023 feet**
Total Elevation Gain:	**1,495 feet**
Parking GPS Coordinates:	**41.25246, -74.05603**
Map:	**NY-NJ TC Northern Harriman- Bear Mountain Trails – Map #119**

Access: Take the Palisades Interstate Parkway to Exit 16, a left-hand exit from the northbound Parkway. When you reach a fork in the road, bear right to continue on Tiorati Brook Road. Proceed 0.5 mile to a parking area on the left-hand side of the road.

Description: The southern ascent of Pingyp Mountain is widely considered to be the most challenging climb on a marked trail in Harriman. Wear sturdy footwear with good traction, hike the loop in the recommended direction (counter-clockwise, as described in this chapter), and choose a day when the rocks are dry and free of snow and ice. By way of comparison, the climb up Pingyp is a bit more difficult than Popolopen Torne (see Chapter 26) but slightly less difficult than Breakneck Ridge in the East Hudson Highlands.

From the parking area, walk east along the right-hand shoulder of Tiorati Brook Road, downhill and back toward the Parkway. Keep right at the fork, following Tiorati Brook Road under the southbound lanes of Lake Welch Drive,

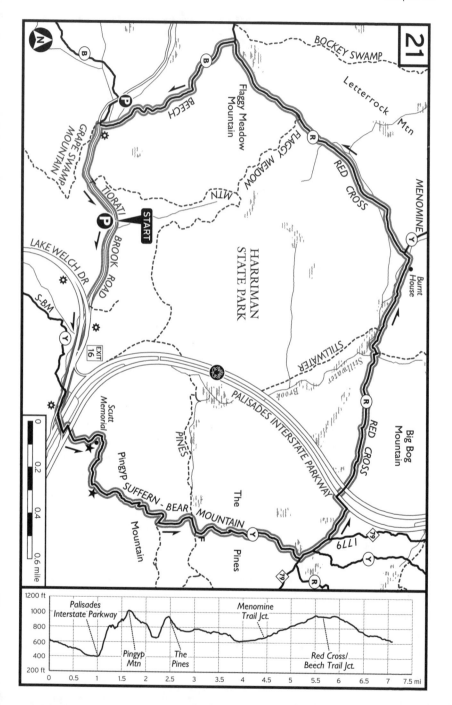

then continue straight at the "yield" sign, merging onto Lake Welch Drive, and bear right at the next fork. In another 0.2 mile, the road crosses a bridge over a stream and is joined by the yellow-blazed Suffern-Bear Mountain (S-BM) Trail, which comes in from the right.

Cross to the left side of the road here and begin following the yellow S-BM blazes (you will be following the S-BM Trail for the next 2.1 miles). The trail bears left at a fork in the road and crosses an overpass that spans the southbound lanes of the Palisades Interstate Parkway. Upon reaching the northbound lanes of the Parkway, the trail turns sharply left, runs along the Parkway for about 125 feet, then crosses the highway (use extreme caution) and begins a steep, rocky climb up Pingyp Mountain.

In the next 0.15 mile, you will climb more than 250 vertical feet. Beyond that point, your climb will become even steeper as you find yourself scrambling up craggy, pitch pine-dotted ledges. On top of the first outcrop, you will find a good southeast-facing view of the Hudson River and Hook Mountain of the Palisades. Just before the next ledge, look for a metal plaque on the rock face, dedicated to the memory of Harold B. Scutt, who was killed in a plane crash in 1930. Five years earlier,

On the way up Pingyp

Climbing the crevice near the summit of Pingyp

in 1925, Scutt scouted about six miles of the S-BM Trail, including this challenging section. You have now traveled one mile.

Now, the trail leads up (and across) a more challenging ledge. Take your time – there are plenty of handholds and footholds, if you look for them. On top, you'll reach a north-facing viewpoint, then swing around to the right and cross two tiny hollows. Next, the trail climbs steeply up a crevice (even more challenging) and then reaches an open ledge with a view. It now descends briefly, then climbs gradually to another rock ledge with a panoramic view. From here, you can see the Hudson River, Stony Point, Haverstraw, Hook Mountain and, to the west, Jackie Jones Mountain. The toughest part of the climb is now behind you.

The trail now goes around a bend, with a view north along the Hudson River. It continues to climb gradually to the summit of Pingyp Mountain, reached at 1.7 miles. Just before arriving at the summit, you'll be treated to one final view, but there are no views from the summit itself, marked by a USGS benchmark on a rock on the left of the trail (elevation 1,023 feet).

The first part of the descent from the Pingyp is moderate, but the descent becomes steeper halfway down, where the trail turns left onto an eroded woods road. At the bottom of the hill, the S-BM briefly turns right onto another woods road. In 300 feet, it turns left, crosses a stream, passes a stone fireplace, and begins a climb of about 250 vertical feet, up a hill known as "The Pines."

Once on top, you will find mountain laurel, chestnut oaks and other hardwoods, but not a single pine tree. Just beyond the summit, a rock ledge affords a glimpse of West Mountain and the Timp, to the north. Here, at 2.5 miles, you have already completed the two most significant climbs of the hike.

After descending from The Pines, the S-BM Trail passes a small, phragmites-filled wetland, then immediately turns left onto a woods road, joining the Red Cross and 1779 Trails. You will be following the Red Cross Trail for the next 2.8 miles. After a few steps, all three trails cross a stream. In another 400 feet, the S-BM Trail leaves to the right, but you should continue ahead, following the co-aligned Red Cross and 1779 Trails.

In another 0.1 mile, at a cairn, the Red Cross and 1779 Trails split. Turn left here, following the Red Cross blazes. After a relatively flat section, the Red Cross Trail reaches the edge of the Palisades Interstate Parkway. Turn left and follow the northbound lanes of the Parkway for about 125 feet, then carefully cross the northbound lanes. The trail continues across the median strip, then turns left for 150 feet and crosses the southbound lanes. On the other side, the trail re-enters the woods, passing through an interesting area of mini-ridgelines, streams and vernal ponds.

View of Jackie Jones Mountain from Pingyp

The trail remains relatively level, keeping to the left of Big Bog Mountain. In about half a mile, it crosses a wet area and then Stillwater Brook on rocks. On the other side of the brook, the Red Cross Trail turns left at a T-intersection, then passes to the right of a pretty wetland, which is often teeming with birds, even in winter. Just past the wetland, at 4.15 miles, a faint old woods road, known as the Stillwater Trail, goes off to the left.

The Red Cross Trail continues along a stream and soon passes to the left of an old cellar hole, identified on the map as the "Burnt House." The home that once stood here was inhabited by a woodcutter named Jonas Lewis and his family. A short distance beyond, the trail turns left and crosses the stream on a wooden bridge. Just beyond the bridge, at 4.45 miles, the yellow-blazed Menomine Trail begins on the right. Note: In case of emergency, there is a trail shelter located 0.85 mile (and 400 vertical feet) up the Menomine Trail.

The Red Cross Trail continues to climb gradually, following a somewhat eroded woods road, sections of which are often very wet. You may have to detour to one side of the road to bypass these wet sections. The trail continues to parallel a branch of the stream, crossing it twice (and also crossing two tributary streams). After passing the start of a faint path, the Flaggy Meadow Mountain Trail, marked

East-facing view from Pingyp

Stone fireplace on the S-BM Trail

by a small cairn on the left, the Red Cross Trail continues on a pleasant footpath through a huge stand of mountain laurels tucked between Flaggy Meadow Mountain (on your left) and Letterrock Mountain (on your right). Just beyond the end of the mountain laurels, you will reach a junction with the blue-blazed Beech Trail, which begins on the left (the junction is marked by a triple blue blaze with the letter "B"). Turn left on the Beech Trail, leaving the Red Cross Trail for good. You have now traveled 5.7 miles.

The Beech Trail heads along the southwestern flank of Flaggy Meadow Mountain, with several wet sections near the start. It rises to the top of a small hill and descends on a woods road, with a few steep sections. Eventually, it begins to parallel the beautiful Tiorati Brook. At 6.6 miles, you will reach paved Tiorati Brook Road. Notice the attractive stone bridge here, which carries the road over the stream. Turn left on Tiorati Brook Road and follow it for 0.5 mile downhill (east) to your car, where the hike began. ⵌ

Chapter 22

Cats Elbow

Rating:	**Moderate**
Distance:	**5.1 miles (5.8 miles with optional side hike)**
Hiking Time:	**3.5 hours (4 hours with optional side hike)**
Attractions:	**Some of the park's best panoramic views, volcanic rock ledges, trail shelter**
Lowest Elevation:	**575 feet**
Highest Elevation:	**1,245 feet**
Total Elevation Gain:	**1,440 feet (1,830 feet with optional side hike)**
Parking GPS Coordinates:	**41.28866, -74.02306**
Map:	**NY-NJ TC Northern Harriman-Bear Mountain Trails – Map #119**

Access: Take the Palisades Interstate Parkway to Exit 17 (Anthony Wayne Recreation Area), which is three miles southwest of the Bear Mountain Bridge. Proceed past the first parking lot, then turn left at a sign for the "Far South Parking Lot," continue through this very large parking lot, and park at the southern end of the lot, near a kiosk and picnic benches. (If the southernmost parking lot is closed, you will have to park at the southern end of the northern parking area, adding about a mile round-trip to your hike.) Most of the time, there is no charge to park at the Anthony Wayne Recreation Area, but there may be a parking charge during special events. When exiting the lot, note that the northbound Parkway is reached from the roadway connecting the north and south lots, while the southbound Parkway is reached from the north end of the northern lot.

Description: From the kiosk at the southern end of the parking area, proceed south on the Horn Hill Bike Path, with blue-on-white diamond blazes, entering a white pine forest. The path is wide and level, but it is winding and there

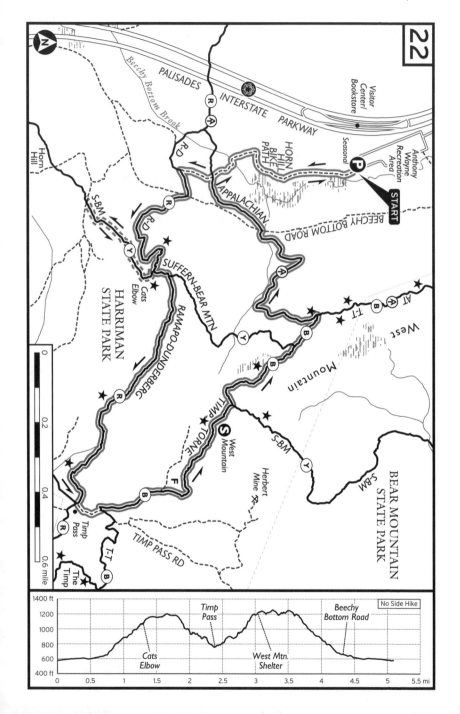

West-facing view from the Cats Elbow

are many exposed tree roots. At 0.2 mile, you'll cross a short wooden bridge (the first of four). At 0.4 mile, the trail turns sharply left and crosses a longer bridge, and a short distance beyond, it crosses a bridge over Beechy Bottom Brook. After crossing a fourth bridge, you'll pass a small knoll on the left and continue across the white-blazed Appalachian Trail. There is a wooden sign at this intersection.

After crossing the Appalachian Trail, be on the lookout for the red-dot-on-white-blazed Ramapo-Dunderberg (R-D) Trail, which intersects the Bike Path in 0.1 mile. Turn sharply left at this junction, leaving the Bike Path, and begin to follow the R-D Trail. You will be following the R-D Trail for the next 1.65 miles.

Proceed uphill on a footpath, then climb stone steps and cross a wide woods road known as Beechy Bottom Road (it is also part of the Bike Path loop). Continue along the R-D Trail, which climbs steadily through dense mountain laurel thickets until it bears left and crosses a gully. The trail now turns left, passes an old mine opening and continues around the side of the mountain. Soon, it turns sharply left, climbs steeply, then follows a level path alongside a cliff, with views to the left.

After climbing steeply to a broad west-facing viewpoint, the trail bears right and continues to climb, soon reaching a panoramic viewpoint at the top of the Cats Elbow. Here, 1.3 miles from the start, the yellow-blazed Suffern-Bear

East-facing view from the Cats Elbow

Mountain (S-BM) Trail joins from the right. This vantage point offers views of the Hudson River, the Palisades and the New York City skyline. Unless you decide to take the side trip mentioned below, turn left, following the co-aligned R-D and S-BM Trails, and skip ahead to the section marked "Hike Continues."

Side Trip: If you just love climbing boulders and are up for the extra workout, this simple out-and-back side trip is for you. Bear right on the yellow-blazed S-BM Trail and make a very steep, 0.35-mile descent down the southwestern flank of West Mountain to an unmarked stone road known as the North "Ski" Trail. Now turn around and scramble back up the S-BM Trail to Cats Elbow. Bear right to continue on the co-aligned R-D and S-BM Trails.

Hike Continues: The R-D and S-BM Trails run together for about 300 feet to a small ledge, where the yellow-blazed S-BM Trail leaves to the left. You should continue straight ahead, following the red-dot-on-white-blazed R-D Trail, which crosses a high, fire-scarred plateau with limited views. As the trail approaches the crest of the rise, you may spot the West Mountain Shelter across the hollow from you. Next, the trail descends briefly and traverses a section of rugged, exposed volcanic rock. There are excellent views of the Timp and the Hudson River from here. The trail now descends rather steeply, with more views along the way.

After crossing an intermittent stream, the trail steeply climbs a rocky slope, turning right at the top. Pay careful attention to the blazes, as this sharp right turn is easy to miss (a very distinct unmarked trail leads to the left here). The R-D Trail continues on a rugged route along the side of a steep slope, soon reaching more viewpoints from rock ledges. Finally, you descend to Timp Pass. Standing in the hollow, you will notice the Red Cross Trail on your right, the R-D Trail proceeding straight ahead, and the unmarked Timp Pass Road on your left. You have now traveled a total of 2.35 miles.

Turn left (north) on Timp Pass Road. In 0.1 mile, watch for the blue-blazed Timp-Torne Trail, which joins Timp Pass Road from the left. Make a sharp left here (do not continue straight on Timp Pass Road) and follow the Timp-Torne Trail up the stone steps. The Timp-Torne Trail will be your route for the next 1.15 miles. The trail immediately turns right and follows an eroded stone road uphill. In 0.25 mile, the Timp-Torne Trail bears right, passes a fireplace, and crosses a brook. The trail now climbs steadily over exposed rocks to the West Mountain Shelter (built in 1928), passing views of the Timp and the Hudson River along the way. You have now traveled 3.05 hilly miles, and this is a good place to break for lunch. The shelter affords panoramic views of the Timp, the Hudson River and the New York City skyline.

After lunch, continue ahead on the blue-blazed Timp-Torne Trail, which now follows a relatively level route. In 500 feet, the yellow-blazed S-BM Trail joins

The Timp and the Hudson River from the R-D Trail

from the right. Bear left here and begin to follow the co-aligned Timp-Torne and S-BM Trails, with blue and yellow blazes. Just ahead on your left are views of the Cats Elbow section of West Mountain, where you hiked earlier in the day. After traversing the highest part of West Mountain, the two trails split at 3.45 miles, where the yellow-blazed S-BM Trail leaves to the left. Continue straight ahead, now once again following only the blue blazes of the Timp-Torne Trail. Soon, views to the west and south will appear.

In another 0.15 mile, you'll reach a T-intersection, marked by a wooden signpost. You'll want to take a break here to enjoy the west-facing views across the Palisades Interstate Parkway and over the hills of Harriman State Park. To your left is Jackie Jones Mountain, with its large communications tower and much smaller fire tower. Straight ahead is Black Mountain – the closest summit from this vantage point.

After taking in the views, turn left, leaving the blue-blazed Timp-Torne Trail, and begin to follow the white-blazed Appalachian Trail (A.T.). Almost immediately, the A.T. begins to descend West Mountain. After following a heavily used and rather eroded trail, with more views to your right, the A.T. continues to descend on a switchback, following a more attractive route constructed in 2014 by

West Mountain Shelter overlooking the Hudson River

Beechy Bottom Road

the Trail Conference Long Distance Trails Crew. The A.T. crosses Beechy Bottom Road (the route of the Bike Path) diagonally to the left at 4.3 miles. Continuing downhill on the A.T., you'll intersect the Bike Path again in 0.2 mile. A wooden sign here points to the right and reads "Bike Path – Parking Lot – 10 Minutes."

Turn right here, retracing your steps along the Bike Path. The Bike Path is sparsely marked in this direction, but it is easy to follow. In 0.6 mile, you'll reach the parking lot where the hike began.

Chapter 23 West Mountain

Rating:	**Moderate to strenuous**
Distance:	**6.45 miles**
Hiking Time:	**4.5 hours**
Attractions:	**Spectacular views of Bear Mountain, the Hudson River and other peaks in Harriman State Park**
Lowest Elevation:	**455 feet**
Highest Elevation:	**1,250 feet**
Total Elevation Gain:	**1,810 feet**
Parking GPS Coordinates:	**41.29779, -74.02710**
Map:	**NY-NJ TC Northern Harriman- Bear Mountain Trails – Map #119**

Access: Take the Palisades Interstate Parkway to Exit 17 (Anthony Wayne Recreation Area). Proceed past a small wooden toll booth (a parking fee may be charged on weekends in the summer if a special event is being held), and immediately turn right into a large parking lot. Turn right again and park towards the north end of the lot.

Description: This hike provides panoramic views of several prominent peaks in Harriman and Bear Mountain parks. Hardwood forests early in the hike give way to a strenuous climb, followed by scenic vistas and interesting rock formations.

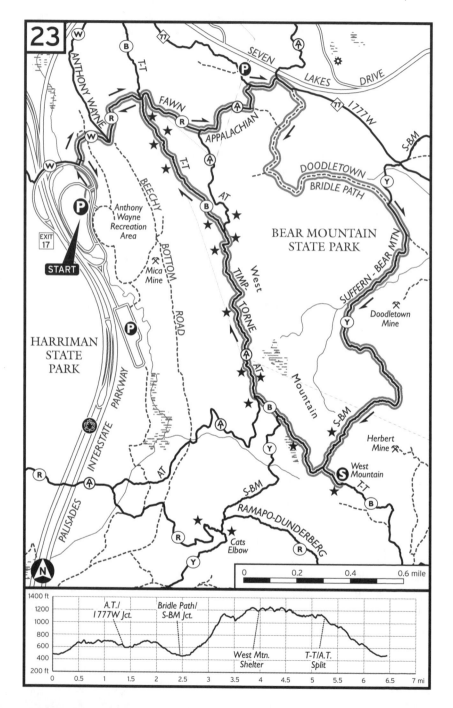

From the parking lot, walk back to the access road and turn left, passing the toll booth. In 500 feet, turn right at a brown metal gate, with stone posts, and head uphill on a gravel road, the route of the white-blazed Anthony Wayne Trail (also the route of the Horn Hill Bike Path). You will pass two small buildings on the left and cross a dirt road.

About 0.2 mile from the gate, you'll reach the dirt Beechy Bottom Road. The Anthony Wayne Trail turns left onto the road, but you should cross the road and a black metal pipe and find a triple red-"F"-on-white blaze, which marks the start of the Fawn Trail. Follow the Fawn Trail up a switchback. The trail continues to climb more gradually, crossing a small stream.

At the height of land, 0.55 mile from the start, the Fawn Trail crosses the blue-blazed Timp-Torne Trail (the junction is marked by a large cairn). If the leaves are down, you'll catch a glimpse ahead of Bear Mountain and the Perkins Memorial Tower. Continue ahead on the Fawn Trail, which now descends.

Cascade on the Doodlekill

In another 0.3 mile, the Fawn Trail ends at the white-blazed Appalachian Trail (A.T.). Continue straight ahead, now following the white blazes of the A.T., which crosses a stream and continues through dense mountain laurel thickets. Soon, the A.T. turns left and descends. At the base of the descent, the A.T. turns right and joins the 1777W Trail. Just before reaching Seven Lakes Drive, the A.T. turns left, but you should turn right onto a gravel road and continue on the 1777W Trail.

In 500 feet, you'll reach a junction, marked by a large number "5" on the left. Turn right here, leaving the 1777W Trail, and proceed uphill on an unmarked woods road, the route of the Doodletown Bridle Path. Historical note: The Doodletown Bridle Path was built as a horse and ski trail in 1935 and was used by horses until the early 1960s. It encircles the former hamlet of Doodletown (which has been unoccupied since 1965). This area is rich in history; in fact, the valley in which Doodletown is located was first settled as early as 1762. A detailed description of the entire Bridle Path can be found in Chapter 35.

You'll pass through an area of pine trees, with many blowdowns from Hurricane Sandy in October 2012. In 0.3 mile, stay on the Bridle Path as it makes a sharp left turn (avoid the less-defined route, which heads right, uphill). After making two more sharp turns, first to the left, then to the right, the Bridle Path heads downhill, overlooking a hollow and a pretty stream on the left. At 2.3 miles, you'll pass a small rock cairn, where the yellow-blazed Suffern-Bear Mountain (S-BM) Trail joins from the left. You'll be following the yellow S-BM blazes for the next 1.55 miles.

The Hudson River and Iona Island from the A.T./T-T along the ridge of West Mountain

In another 750 feet, follow the S-BM Trail as it turns right, leaving the Bridle Path, and crosses a small stream. If there are no leaves on the trees, you'll see a mountain towering ahead. This is a spur of West Mountain, and you'll soon be climbing it! The S-BM Trail begins to climb on a rocky woods road, with detours to avoid eroded sections. It parallels the Doodlekill, then crosses it below an attractive cascade. The climb now steepens, with the trail passing through mountain laurel thickets. This trail section can be very icy and dangerous to navigate in the winter.

After climbing about 500 vertical feet (from the Bridle Path), the trail bears left, leaving the woods road, and continues to ascend more gradually on a footpath. Soon, you'll reach the base of a rocky slope,

Hiker enjoying the view on the ridge of West Mountain

which the trail climbs very steeply. After ascending a little more, you'll go through a cleft in a rock formation at the crest of the rise at 3.25 miles. The trail now descends a little, levels off, and soon turns right. Just beyond, a rock ledge to the left of the trail offers a view through the trees over the Timp and Bald Mountain, with Dunderberg Mountain and the Hudson River beyond.

View of Bear Mountain from the A.T. / T-T along the ridge of West Mountain

The S-BM Trail descends to a hollow and continues through dense mountain laurel thickets. It then steeply climbs a rocky slope to emerge onto an open area with a large boulder and an understory of blueberry. The Perkins Memorial Tower atop Bear Mountain is visible to the right. After descending to cross another hollow, the S-BM Trail climbs to reach a junction, at 3.85 miles, with the blue-blazed Timp-Torne Trail. Turn left here and follow the blue blazes for about 500 feet to the West Mountain Shelter, built in 1928. This is a good place to stop for lunch. The shelter offers excellent views of the Timp and the Hudson River.

When you're ready to continue, retrace your steps on the blue-blazed Timp-Torne Trail to the junction with the S-BM Trail. Turn left at the junction and follow the co-aligned blue and yellow trails. Soon, views open up across the hollow on your left over the Cats Elbow section of West Mountain, with Horn Hill and Big Bog Mountain beyond. You'll pass through an open area and just to the left of the summit of West Mountain. At 4.35 miles, the yellow-blazed S-BM Trail splits off to the left. Continue straight ahead, following the blue blazes of the Timp-Torne Trail.

In another 0.15 mile, you'll reach a signpost at a scenic west-facing viewpoint. Take a moment to gaze out across the Palisades Interstate Parkway and towards the mountains beyond. To your left is Jackie Jones Mountain, with its large communication tower and much smaller fire tower. Straight ahead is Black Mountain, the closest summit from this vantage point. Turn right to continue.

You are now following both the blue-blazed Timp-Torne Trail and white-blazed Appalachian Trail (A.T.). In 0.1 mile, you'll reach an excellent view of Bear Mountain, Anthony's Nose and Iona Island to the northeast.

The next section is an easy-to-navigate, fun-filled tour of West Mountain's western ridgeline. You will find frequent views, a couple of easy rock scrambles, and even an occasional glacial erratic (piece of rock carried by glacial ice and deposited on bedrock of different composition).

After 0.75 mile following blue and white blazes, the trail moves back to the east side of the ridge, with another panoramic view over Bear Mountain. Just beyond, the

Rock outcrop along the Timp-Torne Trail

two trails split. The white-blazed A.T. bears right, but you should bear left to continue on the blue-blazed Timp-Torne Trail, which begins a steady descent. For part of the way, the trail descends on smooth bedrock, which can be quite slippery when wet. After passing through an interesting crevice in the rock, the trail climbs a little to reach a panoramic viewpoint to the west, north and northeast. You might be able to spot your car in the huge Anthony Wayne parking area below on the left, and you'll get a great view of Bear Mountain on the right.

After steeply descending along a rock ledge, you'll reach, at 5.9 miles, a cairn that marks the intersection with the red-"F"-on-white-blazed Fawn Trail. You were here earlier in the hike. Turn left onto the Fawn Trail and follow it 0.25 mile downhill until it ends at Beechy Bottom Road. Continue straight ahead, crossing the black pipe and joining the white-blazed Anthony Wayne Trail, which follows a gravel road downhill. After crossing another dirt road, you'll reach the familiar-looking brown metal gate and paved entrance road. Your car is in the large parking lot just ahead. 🥾

Chapter 24 · Bald Mountain, The Timp and Doodletown

Rating:	**Strenuous**
Distance:	**5.9 miles**
Hiking Time:	**4 hours**
Attractions:	**Spectacular views, deserted village of Doodletown**
Lowest Elevation:	**20 feet**
Highest Elevation:	**1,119 feet**
Total Elevation Gain:	**1,830 feet**
Parking GPS Coordinates:	**41.30108, -73.98599**
Map:	**NY-NJ TC Northern Harriman-Bear Mountain Trails – Map #119**

Access: Take the Palisades Interstate Parkway north to its terminus at the Bear Mountain Circle. Take the first exit off the circle, U.S. Route 9W south, and continue for 1.3 miles to a small hikers' trailhead parking area on the left side of the road, near a wetland and just past a concrete bridge over a stream.

Description: This hike is not exceptionally long, but its length can be deceptive, as it involves a total vertical climb of over 1,800 feet – including a very steep climb of 500 vertical feet in only 0.4 mile.

Begin the hike by carefully crossing Route 9W and finding the blue-blazed Cornell Mine Trail to the left of the bridge over beautiful Doodletown Brook. You will follow the Cornell Mine Trail for the next 1.45 miles. Proceed up a moderately steep rise to a more level area, where you will briefly follow the old Iona Island Aqueduct. Soon, the climb steepens again, and you will pass some pretty cascades on your right before veering left, away from the brook.

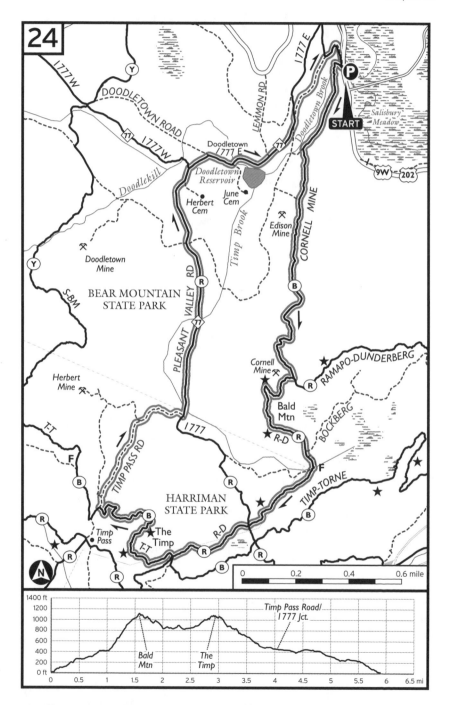

At 0.6 mile, you'll cross a dirt road. If there are no leaves on the trees, you'll be able to see Bald Mountain ahead, towering high above you. Just past the one-mile point, you will begin climbing Bald Mountain in earnest. Pay attention to the blazes, which follow switchbacks up the steep mountain and then continue along an old woods road.

At 1.45 miles, the Cornell Mine Trail ends a junction with the red-dot-on-white-blazed Ramapo-Dunderberg (R-D) Trail. You are now on the crest of the ridge, in a notch between Dunderberg and Bald Mountains. To the right, you will see a small exploratory pit, which is part of the Cornell Mine. For more information on this mine (which includes a 50-foot-long horizontal mine shaft), see *Iron Mine Trails,* by Ed Lenik.

Turn right onto the R-D Trail and follow it up Bald Mountain, passing another mine pit before reaching the summit of the mountain (1,119 feet) – the highest point of the hike. Here, the R-D Trail makes a sharp hairpin turn to the left, but before you turn, you should proceed straight ahead a short distance to open rocks just north of the summit. From this panoramic viewpoint – one of the best in the entire park – you can see Iona Island, the Hudson River and Anthony's Nose, with the Bear Mountain Bridge to the northeast, Bear Mountain (with the Perkins

Bear Mountain Bridge spans the Hudson River to the base of Anthony's Nose, from Bald Mountain

View of Bear Mountain from Bald Mountain

Memorial Tower on its summit) to the northwest, and West Mountain to the west. This is an excellent spot for lunch. When you're ready to continue your hike, be sure to bear right on the R-D Trail.

The trail descends a little, climbs to a south-facing viewpoint, then begins a steady descent. It continues through dense mountain laurel and, after briefly joining a woods road, descends to reach an old stone fireplace along a stream. You have now traveled 2.0 miles (although it will probably seem that you've covered a much greater distance!).

Proceed ahead, following the red-dot-on-white blazes, which cross the stream, bear left from a woods road (do not follow the road downhill to your right), and continue over two low hills. At the top of the second hill, there is a north-facing view from a rock outcrop that looks back over Bald Mountain. The trail now descends to a grassy woods road, the route of the 1777 Trail (marked with white circular blazes with a red 1777).

Cross the 1777 Trail diagonally to the left and continue ahead on the R-D Trail, which soon begins a steady ascent. In 0.3 mile (from the 1777 Trail crossing), just before the crest of the rise, you'll reach an intersection with the blue-blazed Timp-Torne Trail. Turn right, leaving the R-D Trail, and follow the blue blazes toward the Timp, which you'll reach in another 0.2 mile.

The Timp affords a panoramic west-facing view across Timp Pass to West Mountain, with the Hudson River visible to the southeast. This is a popular stop for lunch. Continue along the Timp-Torne Trail for 500 feet to another excellent viewpoint looking across to the Bear Mountain Bridge and Anthony's Nose. This view has appeared in many paintings and photographs over the years.

The Timp-Torne Trail descends, steeply at first, then more gradually. Near the base of the descent, it passes several interesting boulders and reaches a well-defined "stone road," known as Timp Pass Road, in an open area. The Timp-Torne Trail turns left onto Timp Pass Road, but you should turn right and follow the road downhill. In this direction, the road is unmarked, but it is clearly defined and easily followed. You'll pass some huge boulders and towering cliffs. In 0.35 mile, the road bears right and levels off, and in another 0.2 mile, it ends at a junction with another woods road – the 1777 Trail. You have now hiked a total of 4.05 miles.

DAN BALOGH

View of West Mountain from The Timp

Bald Mountain from Pleasant Valley Road

Turn left onto the 1777 Trail, which marks the route followed by British troops under Sir Henry Clinton on October 6, 1777, on their way to attack Forts Clinton and Montgomery. Just ahead, you'll cross a culvert over Timp Brook, with stone foundations and a trail shelter on the right. These are the remnants of a camp once operated by Riverside Church of New York City. Continue ahead on the woods road, now known as Pleasant Valley Road, which goes through the former settlement of Doodletown. This community thrived for two centuries until it was acquired by the park about 1960. Soon, you'll notice white markers that indicate the locations of former homes and other historical sites. From here on, the road is paved, although much of the paving has disintegrated, as the road has been closed to traffic for nearly half a century. (For a detailed history of Doodletown, you may wish to consult *Doodletown: Hiking Through History in a Vanished Hamlet on the Hudson*, by Elizabeth "Perk" Stalter, a former resident of the village, or *Harriman Trails: A Guide and History*, by William J. Myles and Daniel Chazin.)

After about a mile along Pleasant Valley Road (5.0 miles from the start of the hike), the 1777 Trail divides. The 1777W Trail leaves to the left, but you should continue ahead along the road, now following the 1777E blazes. Soon, you'll reach a T-intersection, where Pleasant Valley Road ends. Turn right, now following Doodletown Road. Bear left at the next intersection and

Stone foundation in Doodletown

go around the Doodletown Reservoir (built in 1957). Continue ahead at the following intersection, where Lemmon Road leaves to the left. A short distance beyond, you'll notice a marker to the right, where a path leads down to a waterfall in the stream. Just ahead, the 1777E Trail leaves to the left, but you should continue along the road (now unmarked), which begins a steady descent.

Doodletown historical marker

When you reach a dirt-and-rock barrier across the road, climb over it, and continue ahead as the road makes a sharp turn to the right, with the blue-blazed Cornell Mine Trail joining from the left. The road ends at Route 9W, just north of the parking area where the hike began. 🖅

Chapter 25 Dunderberg-Timp Grand Loop

Rating:	**Strenuous**
Distance:	**6.85 miles (shorter route) or 8.15 miles (longer route)**
Hiking Time:	**5.5 hours or 6.5 hours**
Attractions:	**Spectacular views of Hudson River and surrounding mountains, remains of 19th century spiral railway, including two tunnels, and over 2,200 feet of climbing**
Lowest Elevation:	**15 feet**
Highest Elevation:	**1,119 feet**
Total Elevation Gain:	**2,245 feet (shorter route) or 2,525 feet (longer route)**
Parking GPS Coordinates:	**41.28109, -73.96295**
Map:	**NY-NJ TC Northern Harriman-Bear Mountain Trails – Map #119**

Access: Take the Palisades Interstate Parkway to its northern terminus at the Bear Mountain Circle and proceed south on U.S. Route 9W for about four miles. After climbing a shoulder of Dunderberg Mountain, the road will start a long descent. At the base of the descent, as the road reaches the river level, you'll notice a large parking area on the right. (A side road to Jones Point leaves sharply to the left here.) Park in this gravel parking area.

Alternatively, you can take the Palisades Interstate Parkway to Exit 15 and proceed east on County Route 106 for 2.7 miles to a T-intersection with Route 9W. Turn left and continue for 4.2 miles to a large parking area on the left, opposite the start of the dead-end road to Jones Point on the right (the parking area is 0.2 mile beyond the Anchor Monument).

Description: From the parking area, walk south on Route 9W for 300 feet. Just beyond the Routes 9W and 202 signs, turn right at the trailheads of the Timp-Torne (blue blazes) and Ramapo-Dunderberg (R-D) (red-dot-on-white

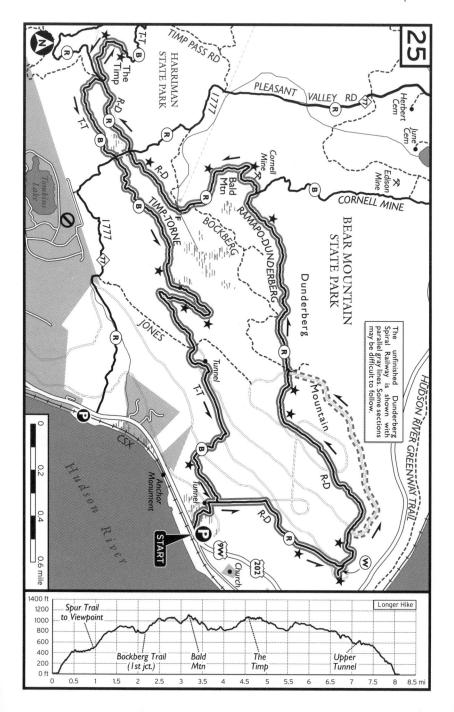

Lower tunnel of Dunderberg Spiral Railway

blazes) Trails. For the most part, you will be following the red-dot-on-white-blazed R-D Trail for the first half of the hike and the blue-blazed Timp-Torne Trail for your return trip.

Follow the coaligned trails on a winding footpath through a level area of vines and brush. At 0.2 mile, the trails climb stone steps, passing a stone-arch tunnel on the left. Take a moment to explore this well-constructed remnant of the ill-fated Dunderberg Spiral Railway. In 1890, construction began on a cable railway designed to carry passengers straight up Dunderberg Mountain using a stationary steam engine. Once on top of the mountain, the train would begin a long, winding, scenic trip downhill, powered by gravity. Although it was never completed, much of the line was graded, and there are two interesting tunnels to explore. The trails now bear right and ascend more steeply on switchbacks and stone steps. At the top of the climb, the blue blazes turn left (your return route), but you should continue straight, climbing steeply on the red-dot-on-white-blazed R-D Trail. Be careful not to twist an ankle on the loose rocks as you climb this section of the old cable incline.

Peekskill across the Hudson River from viewpoint on the R-D Trail

At 0.55 mile, the R-D Trail turns right at a stone abutment and begins to follow a grade of the Dunderberg Spiral Railway. In 0.25 mile, you'll pass a limited viewpoint over the Hudson River to the right, and in another 0.15 mile (one mile from the start of the hike), you'll reach a white-blazed spur trail on your right. Follow this short trail, which leads out to a rock ledge with an expansive view over the Hudson River. The city of Peekskill is visible directly across the river.

Continue on the red-dot-on-white-blazed R-D Trail, which proceeds uphill, passing just to the right of another viewpoint from a rock outcrop on your left. After climbing moderately for about 300 feet beyond this point (at 1.25 miles), you'll notice a small rock cairn on the right, with a footpath leading uphill. Here you must decide whether to take the main route (slightly more strenuous, but you'll be following a blazed and maintained trail) or the alternate Myles View route (not marked or maintained, with some steep drop-offs). Both routes are about the same length.

Main Route (suitable for all hikers): Continue straight ahead, following the R-D Trail up and over the eastern summit of Dunderberg Mountain. The trail goes through a dense forest of young birch trees that are revegetating an area ravaged by a 1999 forest fire. At 2.0 miles, you'll reach a viewpoint over Bear Mountain. The R-D Trail now descends, passes to the right of a small pond and, after climbing slightly to another viewpoint, goes down to a junction with a graded section of the Dunderberg Spiral Railway. Bear right to continue on the R-D Trail, and skip ahead to the section entitled "Hike Continues."

Myles View Option (not suitable for beginners and should not be attemped in wet, snowy or icy conditions): Turn right at the small rock cairn onto the footpath, which climbs the hillside. At the top, bear left and you'll soon emerge onto a grade of the Dunderberg Spiral Railway, which heads north and then curves to the west, following a level route along the northern slope of Dunderberg Mountain. You'll have to climb over some fallen trees, but the route is wide and obvious. In 0.2 mile, you'll reach a series of panoramic north-facing views over Bear Mountain, the Bear Mountain Bridge, the Hudson River, Anthony's Nose and Iona Island. These viewpoints have been named "Myles View" to honor the memory of the late William J. Myles, the author of the authoritative guidebook *Harriman Trails: A Guide and History.*

Soon, the wide railroad grade ends, and you'll continue on a narrow trail along the side of the mountain. Although the footpath is obvious, be careful to watch your step as you proceed over fallen trees and along a steep precipice. After a short distance, the terrain flattens out. Here, the trail route becomes less

Iona Island and the Bear Mountain Bridge from Myles View

obvious, but you should bear right, and you'll soon pass a small phragmites-filled swamp on your left. As you proceed around the right side of the swamp, the railroad grade will begin again. Continue ahead along this wide, clear section of the Dunderberg Spiral Railway grade, passing a large boulder that has fallen into an excavated section of the grade. A few hundred feet beyond, you'll reach an intersection with the red-dot-on-white-blazed R-D Trail. Turn right, rejoining the R-D Trail, and follow the description below in the section "Hike Continues."

Hike Continues: Just beyond the railroad grade, the R-D Trail briefly joins the Bockberg Trail, a woods road. Watch carefully for a double blaze, where the R-D Trail turns right, leaving the Bockberg Trail, and soon passes between two large boulders. The R-D now climbs steadily, with two minor descents, to the summit of Dunderberg Mountain (1,086 feet). Here, 2.9 miles from the start, there are beautiful north-facing views over Bear Mountain from a rock ledge on the right. The trail descends into a notch, passing the end of the blue-blazed Cornell Mine Trail and an exploratory pit on the right at 3.15 miles. Continue along the R-D Trail, which heads uphill to the summit of Bald Mountain (1,119 feet), the highest point of the hike. Here, the R-D Trail makes a sharp hairpin turn to the left, but before you turn, you should check out the excellent views over the Hudson River, the

Hikers at summit of Bald Mountain

Bear Mountain Bridge and Iona Island by proceeding straight ahead a short distance, following an unmarked trail. This is a good spot for lunch. After enjoying the views, be sure to bear right on the R-D Trail to continue your hike.

For the next 0.4 mile, the trail gradually descends, going through thick stands of mountain laurel. After again briefly joining the Bockberg Trail, the trail passes a fireplace on the left and crosses a small stream. Just beyond the stream crossing, follow the red-dot-on-white blazes as they bear left, leaving the road that the R-D Trail has been following (do not follow the road downhill to the right). You have now hiked 3.65 miles.

The R-D Trail now climbs a little, levels off, and then climbs to the top of a rock outcrop, with views back to Bald Mountain. Descending from the rock outcrop, the R-D Trail reaches an intersection (marked by a cairn) with a woods road blazed as the 1777 Trail. Here you must decide whether to take the shorter route (6.85 miles total distance) or to make a super-loop, incorporating the Timp and another picturesque viewpoint (8.15 miles total distance). Note: Chapter 24 will also take you to the Timp.

Shorter Route: Turn left on the 1777 Trail (which uses the route followed by the British to attack Forts Clinton and Montgomery during the Revolutionary War) and proceed for only a few hundred feet to an intersection (also marked by a cairn) with the blue-blazed Timp-Torne Trail. Turn left onto the Timp-Torne Trail and skip ahead to the section marked "Return Trip."

Longer Route (adds 1.3 miles): Cross the 1777 Trail and continue following the R-D Trail. In 0.3 mile, near the top of a steady ascent, the R-D Trail reaches an intersection with the blue-blazed Timp-Torne Trail. Leave the R-D Trail, turn right onto the Timp-Torne Trail, and follow it towards the Timp. (Note: This intersection is easy to miss from this direction. If you begin to descend on the R-D Trail, you have gone too far and should turn around and go back to the intersection, which is clearly visible in the latter direction.) In 0.2 mile, you'll reach the Timp, which offers a beautiful west-facing view across Timp Pass to West Mountain and the surrounding mountains. This is a good place to stop for lunch. You will want to continue 0.1 mile further along the Timp-Torne Trail to another excellent viewpoint looking across to the Bear Mountain Bridge and Anthony's Nose. This view has appeared in many paintings and photographs over the years.

Turn around here, following the Timp-Torne Trail back the way you came. You will pass the Timp and continue ahead until you reach the intersection with the R-D Trail that you encountered earlier. Continue straight ahead on the Timp-Torne Trail, crossing the R-D Trail and soon reaching a southwest-facing view.

Keep following the Timp-Torne Trail as it leads straight ahead across a woods road blazed as the 1777 Trail.

Return Trip (distances based on shorter route): You will be following the blue-blazed Timp-Torne Trail for the next 2.65 miles, all the way back down to Route 9W. The trail ascends gradually, then climbs more steeply on rock steps along a slanted rock slab. After climbing a little more, the trail continues along undulating terrain, then begins a gradual descent, passing a viewpoint over the Hudson River along the way. At 5.1 miles, it switches back to begin making a giant zig-zag down the mountain. Just beyond this sharp right turn, there is a panoramic view over the Hudson River from a rock outcrop on the left. The trail levels off, but after passing a large balanced boulder, it again begins to descend. It then switches back sharply to the left and levels off.

After passing a limited viewpoint in an open area, the trail descends more steeply. At 5.65 miles, it crosses a woods road, known as the Jones Trail, that was built as a work road for the construction of the Dunderberg Spiral Railway. Just beyond, it crosses a small stream and reaches a T-intersection with a graded section of the railway. To the left is a rock cut that leads to one end of an unfinished railway tunnel. The Timp-Torne Trail turns right and follows the railbed, which curves to

Entrance to the upper tunnel of the Dunderberg Spiral Railway

Along the Timp-Torne Trail on the route of the Dunderberg Spiral Railway

the left and traverses a causeway over a low area, then turns left and climbs to the next higher railway grade. Just to the left is the other end of the unfinished tunnel, which was excavated to a depth of about 60 feet. It is often filled with water but can be entered during dry periods. The trail then continues along the railway grade for 175 feet, turns right, and goes down to the next lower grade of the railway. It turns left and follows the lower grade for 0.3 mile until the grade ends. Here, the trail turns right and begins to descend, steeply in places.

At 6.55 miles, you'll reach an intersection with the red-dot-on-white-blazed R-D Trail. You were here near the start of the hike and will now be retracing your steps. Turn sharply right and follow the blue and red-dot-on-white blazes downhill, past the lower tunnel and out to Route 9W. When you reach the road, turn left and follow the road a short distance back to the parking area where the hike began. 🥾

Chapter 26 Popolopen Torne and Gorge

Rating:	**Moderate to strenuous**
Distance:	**4.55 miles (shorter hike) or 5.5 miles (longer hike)**
Hiking Time:	**3.5 hours or 4 hours**
Attractions:	**Views, cascades, lake, rock scrambling**
Lowest Elevation:	**40 feet**
Highest Elevation:	**941 feet**
Total Elevation Gain:	**1,500 feet (shorter hike) or 1,675 feet (longer hike)**
Parking GPS Coordinates:	**41.32405, -73.98772**
Map:	**NY-NJ TC Northern Harriman-Bear Mountain Trails – Map #119**

Access: Take the Palisades Interstate Parkway to its terminus at the Bear Mountain Circle. Proceed north on U.S. Route 9W, cross the viaduct over Popolopen Creek, and immediately turn right into the Fort Montgomery State Historic Site. Park in the lot at the bottom of the ramp.

Description: Although it is only 941 feet above sea level, Popolopen Torne is well worth the trip. It provides a challenging climb up exposed rock faces and the best view of Bear Mountain's rugged north face. Due to its steepness, the Torne should be climbed on a dry, ice-free day. Popolopen Gorge is equally spectacular, featuring rushing rapids at the bottom of a deep, shady gorge.

The hike begins and ends at Fort Montgomery, a destination in itself, featuring historic remains of fortifications from the Revolutionary War. Here, in October 1777, about 700 American soldiers fought unsuccessfully to protect Forts Clinton and Montgomery against 2,100 attacking British and Loyalist troops. Although badly outnumbered, the Patriots' resistance did manage to disrupt

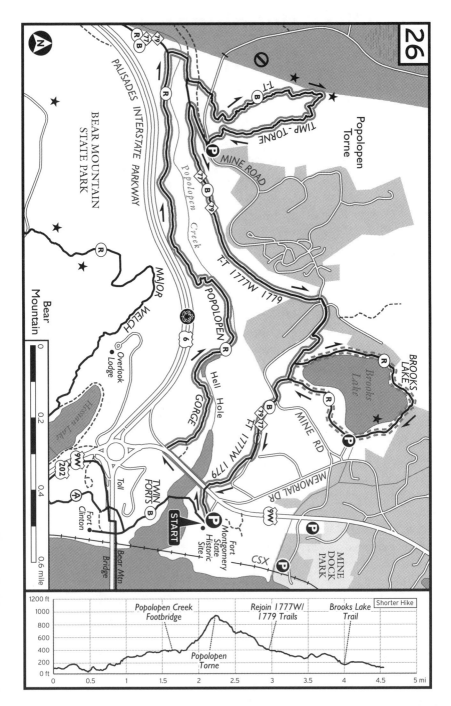

Panoramic view from the Popolopen Viaduct

British plans to control the Hudson River. If you have time, be sure to stop at the Visitor Center and hike down to the suspension footbridge which leads over Popolopen Creek and connects Fort Montgomery with the site of Fort Clinton.

To start the hike, walk back up the ramp you just drove down, toward Route 9W. Without crossing the highway, turn left and walk across the viaduct over Popolopen Creek, enjoying panoramic views to your left. From here, you can see the suspension footbridge, a railroad bridge, and the Bear Mountain Bridge, as well as the Hudson River and the cliffs of Anthony's Nose. At the end of the viaduct and guardrail, turn right and carefully cross Route 9W.

On the west side of Route 9W, find the start of the Popolopen Gorge Trail, marked with three red-square-on-white blazes. The trail descends into Popolopen Gorge on a wide woods road and reaches the abutment of a former bridge across the gorge, overlooking the "Hell Hole" rapids and a dam. The road and bridge were made obsolete by the construction of N.Y. Route 3 (now U.S. Route 9W) and the opening of the Popolopen Viaduct in 1916. The dam, built in 1901, created Roe Pond

Pitch pines on Popolopen Torne

and supplied power to a mill downstream. Next, you will pass Roe Pond and ascend briefly on stone steps. As you pass more rapids, watch for the trail to make a sharp left and begin climbing steeply on stone steps and switchbacks.

At the top of the climb, about a mile from Route 9W, the Popolopen Gorge Trail turns right onto the route of the Bear Mountain Aqueduct, built in 1930 to carry water to the Bear Mountain Inn and rebuilt in 2012. You'll follow the aqueduct through beautiful scenery for the next 0.7 mile (note the manhole covers and exposed sections of pipe from the original 1930 aqueduct). If you hear cars, it is because the Palisades Interstate Parkway is just above you on the left. Keep an eye out on the right for glimpses of the Popolopen Torne through the trees.

After following the aqueduct for about half a mile, you'll come to a fork. The wide woods road – the route of the 2012 aqueduct – bears left here, but the Popolopen Gorge Trail continues straight ahead onto a footpath, following the route of the 1930 aqueduct (now abandoned). In another quarter mile, a woods road joins from the left, and the surrounding area flattens out.

At 1.65 miles, you'll reach a junction with the blue-blazed Timp-Torne Trail, also the route of the 1777W and 1779 Trails. The Popolopen Gorge Trail continues straight ahead, but you should turn right here, leaving the Popolopen Gorge Trail, and head downhill toward the stream, following the Timp-Torne, 1777W and 1779 Trails. At the base of the descent, the trails cross Popolopen Creek on a 62-foot truss footbridge. A footbridge installed here by volunteers of the New York-New Jersey Trail Conference in 2004 was severely damaged by Hurricane Irene in August 2011. In 2013, a new bridge of the same design was procured by the Park and installed by Trail Conference volunteers. After crossing the creek, proceed up the stone steps and turn right on a wide path.

In 300 feet, turn left, following the blue-blazed Timp-Torne Trail, which splits from the 1777W and 1779 Trails. For the next mile, you will follow the Timp-Torne Trail up and then down the Popolopen Torne. Begin climbing, soon crossing the unpaved Fort Montgomery Road and ducking under a guard rail to cross the paved Mine Road. You continue to climb on stone steps and switchbacks. In about 0.15 mile, you'll begin a very steep climb over open rocks, requiring you to use both hands and feet. There are several rock ledges along the way which will allow you to rest and enjoy the fantastic views. Just below the summit, there is a large boulder on your left which provides an excellent view from its top.

Large rock memorial cairn at the summit

The summit – just a few steps ahead – is marked by a large rock cairn dedicated to fallen war heroes and soldiers still fighting overseas. From the open rock ledges, you'll have 360° views of the Hudson River and the Bear Mountain Bridge to the east, Bear Mountain to the south, and the hills of the West Point Military Reservation to the west. You've now hiked 2.2 miles, and you'll want to take a break here to rest from the steep climb and enjoy the panoramic views.

The trail continues straight ahead, descending over rock ledges. Along the way, it first passes a west-facing viewpoint, then swings around and descends to an east-facing rock ledge overlooking the Hudson River, the Bear Mountain Bridge and the East Hudson Highlands. At the bottom of the ledge, the Timp-Torne Trail turns left and descends, steeply at first, then more moderately on switchbacks and stone steps.

At the base of the descent, the trail turns left onto Mine Road. It follows the road for about 100 feet to a small parking area on the right. Turn right at the parking area onto a dirt road and, after passing a sign for the United States Military Reservation, turn left onto a woods road that descends towards the gorge. When you reach a wide woods road, turn left and rejoin the 1777W and 1779 Trails. This road is the route of the 33,000-foot-long West Point Aqueduct, built in 1906. You have now traveled 2.95 miles.

The three co-aligned trails follow the aqueduct for about two-thirds of a mile, rising to a high point, then descend to cross a stream on rocks. After a brief

East-facing view from Popolopen Torne

West-facing view from Popolopen Torne

ascent, the trails reach the paved Mine Road. Turn right and walk along the road for about 500 feet (passing Wildwood Ridge, a dead-end street), then follow the three trails as they turn left, leaving Mine Road, and descend along the hillside on a footpath. The body of water below you is Brooks Lake.

At 3.95 miles, you'll reach a junction with the red-square-on-white-blazed Brooks Lake Trail (not to be confused with the Popolopen Gorge Trail, also blazed red-on-white, which you followed earlier in the hike). If you wish to return to your car by the most direct route, choose the "Shorter Hike." If you wish to circle Brooks Lake, adding about a mile to your hike, skip ahead to the section marked "Longer Hike."

Shorter Hike: Bear right, continuing to follow the Timp-Torne, 1777W and 1779 Trails (now also joined by the Brooks Lake Trail) as they cross a wet area on puncheons. In about 100 feet, the Brooks Lake Trail leaves to the left, and you should bear right to continue on the Timp-Torne, 1777W and 1779 Trails. Skip ahead now to the section marked "Return Trip."

Longer Hike: Turn left onto the red-square-on-white-blazed Brooks Lake Trail, which circles Brooks Lake in a clockwise direction. In 0.25 mile, you'll cross a stream and, in another 125 feet, you'll pass a rock on your right with a nice view

Brooks Lake

over the lake. In another third of a mile, the trail comes out onto a grassy area (a town park), passes a wooden pavilion, and terminates (for now) at a parking lot. Proceed across the lot to find the triple-blazed start of the Brooks Lake Trail, and continue along the Brooks Lake Trail as it proceeds south around the lake. It follows a wide fire road for about 125 feet, then turns left and continues on a narrower gravel road.

After a short descent, about 0.3 mile from the parking lot, the Brooks Lake Trail reaches a junction with the Timp-Torne, 1777W and 1779 Trails. Proceed straight ahead here (do not turn right), leaving the Brooks Lake Trail, and rejoining the Timp-Torne, 1777W and 1779 Trails. Continue with the section marked "Return Trip."

Return Trip: Stay on the coaligned Timp-Torne, 1777W and 1779 Trails for the final half-mile of your hike. In 0.1 mile, the trails turn left onto Mine Road. They follow the road for only 150 feet, then turn right, leaving the paved road, and descend on an old woods road. The trails bear left at a fork and climb an embankment to emerge onto a paved road. Take the right fork and head slightly downhill along the road for about 275 feet. The three trails now turn right, leaving the road, and reenter the woods. They continue under Route 9W to the Fort Montgomery Historic Site, where the hike began. 🥾

Chapter 27 Bear Mountain

Rating:	**Strenuous**
Distance:	**4.9 miles**
Hiking Time:	**3.5 hours**
Attractions:	**Historic landmarks, panoramic views, starkly contrasting conditions, challenging descent on the Major Welch Trail**
Lowest Elevation:	**155 feet**
Highest Elevation:	**1,290 feet**
Total Elevation Gain:	**1,520 feet**
Parking GPS Coordinates:	**41.31271, -73.98892**
Map:	**NY-NJ TC Northern Harriman-Bear Mountain Trails – Map #119**

The 5,067-acre Bear Mountain State Park was first established in 1913, but its historical and military significance dates back to the American Revolution. Today, the park offers hiking, biking, boating, picnicking, swimming, cross-country skiing, sledding and ice-skating, as well as a zoo, a trailside museum, a carousel, overnight accommodations and a dining facility. Since it welcomes more visitors each year than Yellowstone National Park, it can be crowded on weekends.

To fully appreciate Bear Mountain, which towers over the Hudson River and the surrounding landscape, one should view it from all sides. Hiking the loop in the direction described in this hike yields superior views; however, care should be taken when descending the north face of the mountain on the Major Welch Trail, especially if the trail is wet or covered with snow or ice.

Access: Take the Palisades Interstate Parkway to its northern terminus at the Bear Mountain Circle. Take the first exit onto U.S. Route 9W south (do not cross the Bear Mountain Bridge). Follow Route 9W for about half a mile, bear right

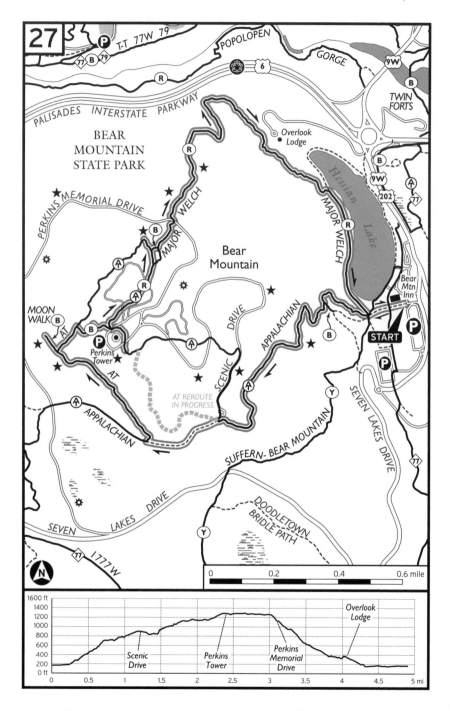

Iona Island and the Hudson River from the A.T. on the way up Bear Mountain

at the first traffic light, and turn right onto the circular drive in front of the Bear Mountain Inn. After passing in front of the Inn, turn right into the large parking lot between the Inn and the Administration Building (a parking fee is charged on weekdays in the summer and on weekends year round).

Description: From the parking lot, proceed across the lawn to the southwest corner of the Bear Mountain Inn. The Inn was constructed in 1914-15 of native stone and chestnut logs and was reopened to the public in 2012 following an extensive six-year renovation. Continue west (toward the mountain) on a paved path. About 400 feet beyond the Inn, you'll reach a junction of paved paths, marked by a trail sign. Bear right, following the white blazes of the Appalachian Trail (A.T.) as it leaves the paved path toward a stone building known as the Spider Hill House.

You are now following the new route of the A.T., a marvel of stonework constructed over a five-year period by Trail Conference volunteers, along with skilled and experienced professional trail builders. This trail segment has been constructed to sustain the impact of the many thousands of feet that annually make their way up this popular route. More than 800 individuals volunteered over 30,000 hours of their time to construct this spectacular trail section. As you climb the steps to the Scenic Drive, you will appreciate the work it took to cut, place and anchor the granite slabs into place.

The A.T. climbs through an interesting section of large boulders before reaching a junction with a blue-blazed trail, which begins on the left. This blue-blazed trail heads back towards the Bear Mountain Inn, but you should bear right to continue along the A.T.

After going around more boulders, the trail bears left and crosses a 28-foot-long wooden bridge. A short distance beyond, the trail reaches a viewpoint over Iona Island and the Hudson River. Continue to climb past a seasonal waterfall (above on the right) and through an area known as the "pine flats."

At 1.25 miles (after climbing 715 steps, with 730 feet of elevation gain), you will emerge onto a paved road, known as the Scenic Drive. The A.T. turns right onto the paved roadway, but you should turn left, passing a circle at the end of the drivable road and continuing on an abandoned stretch of the Scenic Drive. The old roadway offers a pleasant walk alongside the cliffs of Bear Mountain's southern face. In a quarter mile, you'll reach a junction with another section of the white-blazed A.T. Here, the A.T. blazes lead both straight ahead and sharply to the right. You should make the sharp hairpin turn to the right (do not continue straight ahead along the road) and immediately climb an impressive set of stone steps. The A.T. continues its climb toward the summit, with increasingly expansive south-facing views.

At 2.0 miles (after climbing another 300 steps), the A.T. reaches a junction with a blue-blazed spur trail, marked by a cairn in the middle of a large rock slab. Bear left and follow the blue-blazed trail (the blue blazes are painted on the rocks and may be difficult to follow if the ground is covered with snow). This trail section (formerly part of the Major Welch Trail) is often referred to as the Moon Walk. Notice that the bare rocks have an unusual orange hue, similar to those found on parts of Diamond Mountain (see Chapter 4). In about 500 feet, the blue trail ends at an impressive west-facing viewpoint. Return as you came and, when you reach the A.T., make sure to turn left, following the white blazes (do not continue straight).

In another 400 feet, leave the A.T. and turn right onto another blue-blazed trail. Follow this trail uphill for 0.15 mile until it ends just before the paved Perkins Memorial Drive. Continue straight, now following the white-blazed A.T. and red-ring-on-white Major Welch Trail. The trail immediately crosses the road and reaches the Perkins Memorial Tower at 2.4 miles. The tower, which is well worth a visit when open, was built as a memorial to George W. Perkins, Sr., the first president of the Palisades Interstate Park Commission. Inside and up the steps, you will find historic exhibits and panoramic views of four states, the Hudson River valley and New York City.

Stone steps climbing Bear Mountain on the Appalachian Trail

The Moon Walk on Bear Mountain

West Point boundary monument

After viewing the exhibits and taking in the views, cross the Perkins Memorial Drive again and continue to a panoramic overlook, with magnificent views to the south, east and west. Now retrace your steps on the A.T. across Perkins Memorial Drive and continue ahead on the A.T. and the Major Welch Trail. For the next third of a mile, you will be following a beautiful, expertly designed wheelchair-accessible trail, which allows all users to explore the summit area.

In 600 feet, the co-aligned A.T. and Major Welch Trails cross a gravel service road, then pass just to the left of a massive boulder, where the true summit of Bear Mountain is located. If you climb the giant rock, you will find small concrete foundations and steel rods – the remnants of a fire tower which was removed when Perkins Tower was built in 1934. Continue past another huge boulder (on your left), then bear left at the fork, now following only the white A.T. blazes. Continue past the blue-blazed spur trail on your right to the end of the handicapped-accessible trail at a beautiful viewpoint to the north and west. Just below, you will see a five-foot-high stone boundary monument. This monument marked the boundary between the Park and the West Point Military Reservation until 1942, when the Park obtained ownership of this wedge-shaped section of the mountain in a land swap with West Point.

Now retrace your steps and follow the A.T. back to the blue-blazed spur trail. Turn left and follow the blue blazes a few hundred feet to the Major Welch Trail. Turn left onto the Major

Perkins Memorial Tower

Welch Trail (with red-ring-on-white blazes), which you will follow all way back to the Bear Mountain Inn. The trail is quite steep in places, but it features a series of spectacular north-facing views overlooking Popolopen Torne, Brooks Lake, Fort Montgomery, the Hudson River and West Point.

Historical Note: The Major Welch Trail is named for Major William Addams Welch (1868-1941), who served as the Chief Engineer and General Manager of the Palisades Interstate Park Commission for 26 years. He was known as "the father of the state park movement" and was instrumental in developing Harriman and Bear Mountain State Parks, constructing lakes, camps and scenic roads (including Storm King Highway and the original Seven Lakes Drive). He was a founder of

Hessian Lake with Anthony's Nose in the background across the Hudson River

the Palisades Interstate Park Trail Conference, which became the New York-New Jersey Trail Conference, and he served as Chairman of the Appalachian Trail Conference (now the Appalachian Trail Conservancy).

At 3.1 miles, you will cross the Perkins Memorial Drive diagonally to your left and descend over a steep retaining wall. The trail now leads down a steeply sloped rock face to another outstanding view from a pretty pitch pine-dotted rock outcrop. This is a good place to stop for a break.

Soon, you'll go down another steep rock face. If you wish, you might be able to find an easier way down by keeping to the left or the right of the rock. Notice the difference in sunlight, vegetation, temperature and wind conditions here on the north face of the mountain, as compared to the brighter, south-facing side.

About half a mile beyond the last crossing of the Perkins Memorial Drive, the Major Welch Trail turns right onto a well-graded footpath, with stone steps. This beautiful trail section was constructed in the spring of 2013 by the Jolly Rovers volunteer trail crew of the Trail Conference, together with AmeriCorps interns. In about 600 feet, the trail turns left at a large boulder and descends a long flight of narrow stone steps wedged between large rocks, then bears left and switches back towards the east.

At the end of the switchback, the trail turns right and descends more steeply. It bears right at the base of the descent and follows a relatively level but very rocky footpath. After passing Overlook Lodge (below on your left) and a water tower (above on your right), the trail finally descends to a paved path that runs along the shore of Hessian Lake.

Turn right on the path and follow it for 0.4 mile, passing some impressive boulders. Continue past a boathouse and the southwest corner of the lake to the end of the Major Welch Trail at a junction with the A.T. You have now completed your hike loop and hiked a total of 4.75 miles. To return to your car, turn left and follow the paved path alongside the Bear Mountain Inn to the parking lot where the hike began. 🖊

Trail Runs, Walks, Ski Loops and Mountain Bike Rides

Walkers, hikers, trail runners, mountain bikers and cross-country skiers are kindred spirits. Each of us shares a common love of nature, physical exercise and adventure. We are bonded by our choice to use "human power," not engine power, to fuel our enjoyment of the outdoors. The following chapters are all suitable for those who choose to walk or trail run. Two of the loops may also be skied, and one is approved for mountain bikes.

Just as we respect our environment, we are called upon to respect our fellow trail users. The best way to do this is simply to pay attention and leave plenty of space between yourself and slower moving traffic. If you are coming up behind someone, announce your presence in advance. If you intend to pass, indicate the side on which you will be passing.

About Trail Running

Runners are taking to the woods as never before. As people discover the benefits of training in nature and on natural surfaces, trail runners in Harriman-Bear Mountain parks are an increasingly common sight. In addition to its cardiovascular and psychological benefits, trail running reduces repetitive motion injuries (as compared to road running) and actively engages the core and stabilizer muscles. Those who have tried the sport understand the feeling of exhilaration that comes from experiencing the forest in this unique way.

Runners (and cross-country skiers) generally prefer a less rocky route than many hiking trails offer. Serious athletes may also desire a very smooth section of trail to temporarily increase pace, heart rate and foot turnover. A long stretch of woods road, which might be less interesting to hikers, can be a highly desirable feature on a trail run. Hills are welcomed as part of the challenge, but extremely steep climbs are best left for hikers. Runners tend to derive the greatest training benefit from continuous running and faster foot turnover.

If you are new to trail running, plan to ease into it slowly. Try jogging only the smoothest and flattest sections of trail at first. Ankle twists are common among beginners, so consider starting in shoes with ankle support, running shorter loops, and running with a partner. You do not want to find yourself injured and alone out on the trail. Consume sports drinks with electrolytes before, during and after your run. Tell another person where you are going and when you expect to return. Bring a cell phone, but realize that you may not have reception in all areas of the park.

Take your time, and use caution the first time you explore a new running route. Treat it as a scouting trip, and carry this book with you. Do not expect an uninterrupted, quality run until you have become completely familiar with the route and all its turns. Navigation can be tricky at first, but once you have mastered a route, it will be yours to enjoy for life. ℟

Chapter 28 Lakes Sebago and Skenonto

Type:	**Trail run or walk**
Distance:	**6.35 miles**
Attractions:	**Two scenic lakes, a good hill workout, easy access from major highways**
Lowest Elevation:	**530 feet**
Highest Elevation:	**1,010 feet**
Total Elevation Gain:	**940 feet**
Parking GPS Coordinates:	**41.18015, -74.16351**
Map:	**NY-NJ TC Southern Harriman-Bear Mountain Trails – Map #118**

Access: Take N.J. Route 17 north to the New York State Thruway and take the first exit, Exit 15A (Sloatsburg). Turn left at the bottom of the ramp onto N.Y. Route 17 north, and continue through the village of Sloatsburg. Just beyond the village, turn right at the next traffic light, following the signs for Seven Lakes Drive and Harriman State Park. Cross an overpass over railroad tracks and continue along Seven Lakes Drive for 0.7 mile, passing under the New York State Thruway. Just before reaching a large sign "Welcome to Harriman State Park," turn left at a sign for Johnsontown Road, immediately reaching a stop sign at a T-intersection. Turn right, proceed for 1.2 miles to the end of the road, and park along the right side of the circle.

Description: Begin by walking to the northeastern end of the cul-de-sac, exactly halfway around the circle. Your run starts at the trailhead of the White Bar Trail, marked by a triple horizontal white blaze. Follow the blazes uphill to the northeast on a grassy woods road (Old Johnsontown Road). In 0.3 mile, the vertical white blazes of the Kakiat Trail briefly join from the left then depart to the right.

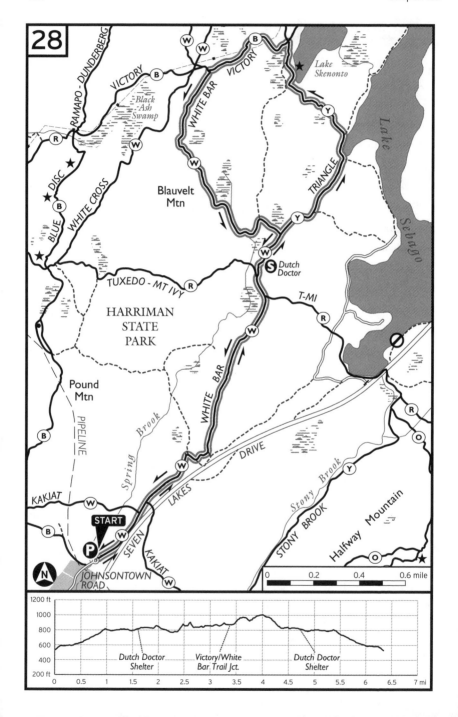

Lake Sebago

In another 0.15 mile, after climbing some more, the White Bar Trail turns left, passes some boulders, then turns right at a fork. Continue to follow the horizontal white blazes. At 0.65 mile, the trail turns left, passing two green metal gateposts, and continues its climb. In another half mile, the trail begins to descend toward a marshy area. About 1.5 miles from the start, the red-square-on-white-blazed Tuxedo-Mt. Ivy Trail joins from the right and, in 500 feet, leaves to the left. Bear right at the fork to continue along the White Bar Trail. Just beyond, you'll pass the Dutch Doctor Shelter on your right.

At 1.75 miles (0.15 mile beyond the shelter), the White Bar Trail turns left, but you should continue straight ahead on the Triangle Trail (blazed with yellow triangles), which you will follow for the next 1.15 miles. Continue through a pretty stretch of mountain laurel (disregard the various unmarked side trails) and in half a mile, you'll reach the shore of Lake Sebago. The Triangle Trail crosses a tiny inlet on rocks, follows the shoreline for a short distance, then turns left and goes over two ridges, which can be challenging to run. Watch your footing, especially as you descend and cross an inlet to Lake Skenonto (which is now visible on your right).

Suddenly, the Triangle Trail turns right at a rock slab – a turn that is very easy to miss. You can either turn right here or, if you miss the turn, simply go straight until you reach a woods road in less than 250 feet. Turn right on the woods road and you will soon rejoin the yellow blazes of the Triangle Trail, which comes in on your right. In another 250 feet, you'll reach an intersection with the

Lake Skenonto

Victory Trail, a woods road blazed with a blue "V" on a white background. Turn left (southwest) onto the Victory Trail, leaving the Triangle Trail.

Follow the Victory Trail for the next 0.45 mile, twice crossing under power lines. After the second power line crossing, watch closely on your left for a junction with the White Bar Trail (marked with horizontal white blazes) – the same trail you followed earlier – at a curve to the right on the Victory Trail. Turn left onto the White Bar Trail. You have now traveled 3.35 miles, and you'll be following the White Bar Trail for the remaining 3.0 miles back to your car.

Proceed uphill on the White Bar Trail, with the Black Ash Swamp visible below on your right. This is a moderately challenging climb which tops out at just over 1,000 feet – the highest elevation on this hike. Descend carefully from the crest of the rise, watching for rough terrain and a stream crossing near the base of the descent. At 4.6 miles, you'll pass the yellow-blazed Triangle Trail on your left, followed by the Dutch Doctor Shelter.

If this section of the trail looks familiar, it's because you followed this exact route earlier on the hike, albeit in the reverse direction. You will soon pass the red-square-on-white-blazed Tuxedo-Mt. Ivy Trail, the marsh and the green gates. Remember that the trail makes a brief zig-zag around some boulders. The final half-mile leads straight downhill to Johnsontown Circle and your car. 🚶

Chapter 29 Lake Stahahe

Type:	**Trail run or walk**
Distance:	**6.35 miles**
Attractions:	**Scenic lake and brook, summer camps, beautiful views of surrounding mountains**
Lowest Elevation:	**550 feet**
Highest Elevation:	**830 feet**
Total Elevation Gain:	**935 feet**
Parking GPS Coordinates:	**41.26475, -74.15434**
Map:	**NY-NJ TC Northern Harriman-Bear Mountain Trails – Map #119**

If you enjoy running along water, this beautiful lollipop-loop hike is for you. For part of the way, you'll follow Arden Road (also known as the Old Arden Road), which was built by the Harriman family to connect their home, the Arden Estate, with the village of Tuxedo. Lake Stahahe derives its name from the Mohegan word meaning "stones in the water." It is a natural lake that was enlarged by dams. Be advised that you will encounter two rough patches, one along Stahahe Brook and the other along the west side of Lake Stahahe. Sections of this loop do not follow official blazed trails, and some portions of the hike are on paved surfaces.

Please note that the route of this hike passes by several youth camps that are actively used each summer. The camps are strictly off-limits when campers are present, so you are requested not to hike or run this loop during the summer months, when the camps are in session.

Access: Take N.J. Route 17 north to the New York State Thruway and take the first exit, Exit 15A (Sloatsburg). Turn left at the bottom of the ramp onto

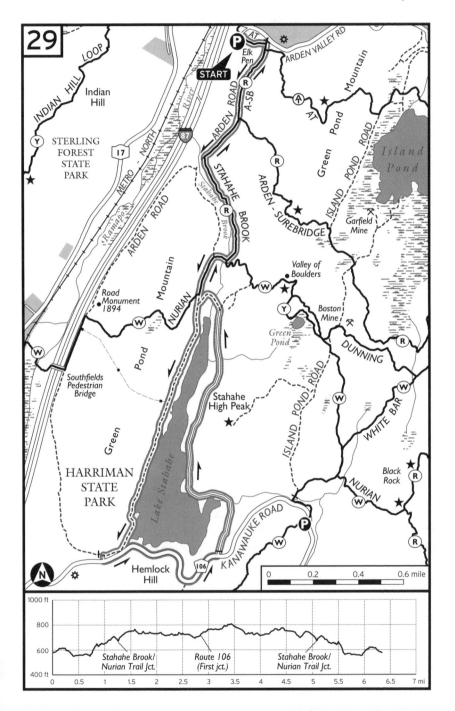

Elk Pen

N.Y. Route 17 north and continue through the villages of Sloatsburg, Tuxedo and Southfields. About two miles north of Southfields, turn right onto Arden Valley Road just beyond a "Welcome to Harriman State Park" sign. Cross the bridge over the New York State Thruway, then make the first right into the Elk Pen parking area.

Description: From the east side of the parking area, proceed east on the white-blazed Appalachian Trail, which crosses a grassy meadow and heads toward the forested hills. At the edge of the woods, turn right onto a woods road, known as Arden Road, built by Edward Harriman in the 1890s. Soon, the Appalachian Trail leaves to the left, but you should continue ahead on Arden Road, now following the inverted-red-triangle-on-white blazes of the Arden-Surebridge (A-SB) Trail. You are proceeding south, along the edge of the forest. The "Elk Pen" in the field below was home to a herd of elk brought in from Yellowstone National Park in 1919. The elk did not thrive, and the few survivors of the herd were sold by the Park in 1942.

About half a mile from the start, the A-SB Trail leaves to the left, but you continue straight ahead on Arden Road, now following the red-stripe-on-white blazes of the Stahahe Brook Trail. After descending gradually for 0.3 mile, you'll reach Stahahe Brook. The road formerly crossed the brook on a wood-and-stone bridge, but the bridge was washed out by Hurricane Irene in August 2011, and the Park has decided not to replace it. Turn left and continue to follow the

Stahahe Brook Trail, beginning the most extensive climb of the trip – a rough, multi-tiered ascent totaling 190 vertical feet. In half a mile, you'll reach the southern end of the Stahahe Brook Trail. Turn right and follow the white-blazed Nurian Trail, which crosses two branches of Stahahe Brook on rocks, then bears left and heads south on a woods road.

In a quarter mile, you'll reach a fork. Here, the Nurian Trail bears right and leaves the woods road, but you should continue ahead on the road. Just beyond, another road joins from the left. Continue ahead on a flat, smooth, semi-paved road, keeping Lake Stahahe on your left. As Green Pond Mountain begins to rise steeply to your right, the road will disappear, and your path will become narrow and scant. Be careful here. You will be joined by a metal pipe and rubber water hose, which will conspire against you to make running difficult. While annoying, this section does not last for long. The pipe and hose eventually veer away from the shore uphill, but you should continue to hug the shore. You'll pass a dock on your left, and you may have to jump over some fallen trees before the ragged path along the shore of the lake becomes clear again. The rest of your run should go smoothly.

After ascending past some old cabins (keep to the left of the cabins), you will pass a large maintenance building and join a paved road. Follow the road past a park building and continue straight ahead to the paved Route 106 (Kanawauke Road). Turn left on Route 106 (Kanawauke Road), following the left shoulder uphill for half a mile. Take the first left onto a paved road which follows the eastern shore of the lake. This little-traveled road will take you past several summer camps. Continue following the main road, keeping the lake on your left, until you reach the northern tip of the lake. Here, you will reach a fork at the end of the paved road.

Bear left at the fork, swinging around the tip of the lake and crossing Stahahe Brook. In about 500 feet, watch closely for a very sharp right turn. Turn right here onto the same unpaved road you followed on your way to the lake. You have now traveled 4.85 miles. Almost immediately, the white blazes of the Nurian Trail come in from the left. You should now begin to follow the white-blazed Nurian Trail. In a quarter mile, after recrossing

Stone building along Lake Stahahe

Lake Stahahe

Stahahe Brook, bear left onto the red-stripe-on-white-blazed Stahahe Brook Trail. The trail descends gradually at first, then more steeply.

In half a mile, you'll reach Arden Road. Turn right onto the road, continuing to follow the Stahahe Brook Trail. When you reach the end of the Stahahe Brook Trail in 0.3 mile, continue ahead on the road, now following the inverted-red-triangle-on-white-blazed A-SB Trail. In another 0.35 mile, the white-blazed Appalachian Trail joins, and just beyond, it turns left. Follow the Appalachian Trail across the meadow and back to your car at the Elk Pen parking area. 🚶

Chapter 30 Island Pond

Type:	**Trail run or walk**
Distance:	**4.95 miles (shorter hike) or 6.95 miles (longer hike)**
Attractions:	**Scenic lake, wetlands, cascade**
Lowest Elevation:	**900 feet**
Highest Elevation:	**1,160 feet**
Total Elevation Gain:	**800 feet (shorter hike) or 1,070 feet (longer hike)**
Parking GPS Coordinates:	**41.23488, -74.14906**
Map:	**NY-NJ TC Northern Harriman-Bear Mountain Trails – Map #119**

The first half of this beautiful loop is on hiking trails. Be prepared for some rugged sections, a number of stream crossings and one very wet section (at the south end of Island Pond). Unless you do not mind getting wet, you should wait for dry conditions before attempting this one.

Around the halfway point, you will have the option to take a scenic out-and-back trip to a waterfall. This side trip, on smooth gravel and paved roads, is ideal for adding a tempo run or strides in the middle of your workout. Similar conditions can also be found on the final 1.2 miles of the loop.

Access: Take N.J. Route 17 north to the New York State Thruway and take the first exit, Exit 15A (Sloatsburg). Turn left at the bottom of the ramp onto N.Y. Route 17 north, and continue through the villages of Sloatsburg and Tuxedo. About 2.2 miles beyond the village of Tuxedo, bear left at a traffic light at the intersection of N.Y. Route 17A. At the top of the ramp, turn right onto County Route 106 (Kanawauke Road), crossing over Route 17 and then going under

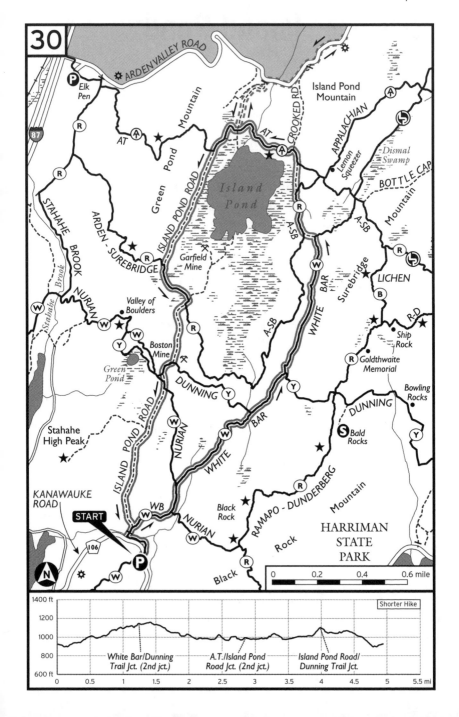

Shorter Hike

White Bar/Dunning
Trail Jct. (2nd jct.)

A.T./Island Pond
Road Jct. (2nd jct.)

Island Pond Road/
Dunning Trail Jct.

Island Pond

the New York State Thruway. Continue for about 2.2 miles to the first parking area on the right side of the road. The parking area, which is past Lake Stahahe (visible through trees to the left), is just beyond a sharp curve in the road.

Description: At the western edge of parking area, find the horizontal white blazes of the White Bar Trail, and follow them north across Route 106 (Kanawauke Road). You'll be following the White Bar Trail for the next 1.85 miles, although several other marked trails will briefly join your route.

After crossing Route 106, the trail curves left and descends, paralleling the road for about 500 feet. It then turns right onto a woods road and crosses over a stream. A short distance beyond, you'll come to a fork, where you should bear right to continue along the White Bar Trail. The trail ascends gently through a mixed hardwood forest for a quarter mile before another white-blazed trail, the Nurian Trail, joins from the right. Note: The blazes of the Nurian Trail are vertical, rather than horizontal.

Continue ahead on the joint White Bar/Nurian Trail. In 500 feet, the Nurian Trail departs to the left, and you should bear right to continue on the White Bar Trail (horizontal white blazes). Expect to encounter rugged trail conditions and some stream crossings for the next 1.5 miles. In another half mile, the yellow-blazed Dunning Trail joins from the left, and you will again be following two co-aligned trails. Pay close attention as you approach a tiny stream in another quarter mile. Here, the yellow-blazed Dunning Trail continues straight, but you should turn left, crossing the stream and continuing on the White Bar Trail. This turn is easy to miss, especially if you are running.

The White Bar Trail now follows the route of an old miners' road, known as the Crooked Road. It climbs briefly, then descends and crosses a stream. At 1.85 miles (0.6 mile beyond where you left the yellow-blazed trail), you'll come to a fork. Here, the White Bar Trail turns right, but you should bear left to continue along the Crooked Road, now unmarked. After descending for about 100 feet and crossing a wet area, the inverted-red-triangle-on-white blazes of the Arden-Surebridge (A-SB) Trail join from the left.

Soon, the A-SB Trail crosses a stream on rocks. This stream, which may be difficult to cross during periods of high water, flows from Dismal Swamp on the right to Island Pond, now visible on your left. Pay attention, because in

Stone spillway along the A.T. near Island Pond

another 0.15 mile, you will reach another fork. The A-SB turns right, heading uphill, but you should bear left, continuing on the unmarked Crooked Road. As of this writing, there is a large fallen tree across the Crooked Road just beyond this junction. Follow the Crooked Road downhill and, in another 0.15 mile, the white-blazed Appalachian Trail (A.T.) joins from the right. You'll be following the A.T. for the next 0.4 mile.

Just beyond the north end of Island Pond, follow the A.T. as it turns left, leaving the Crooked Road, and climbs a small hill which offers a nice view of Island Pond, on your left. The A.T. now descends, passes the rusted remains of a rotary gravel classifier, then crosses a stone spillway and climbs to a gravel road. You've now traveled 2.7 miles. If you wish to do the shorter (4.95-mile) run, proceed straight across the road, still following the A.T., and skip ahead to the section entitled "Return Trip."

Longer run (out-and-back spur): For a longer run, do not cross the gravel road. Instead, turn right onto the road, leaving the A.T. for now. Continue north for a quarter mile, passing to the right of a green/white gate and reaching paved Arden Valley Road. Turn right on Arden Valley Road, a rolling, forested route which is closed to vehicles during the wintertime and lightly traveled the rest of the year. Pay attention to this junction so you will recognize it when you return to it later.

Follow Arden Valley Road east, watching for any traffic. In 0.7 mile, you will reach an attractive cascade on your right. Assuming that you turn back here, the total distance of your run will be 6.95 miles. Note: Arden Valley Road continues as a quiet, paved, rolling road for another 2.8 miles, finally terminating at a busy traffic circle by Lake Tiorati. However far you venture on Arden Valley Road, return exactly as you came, making sure not to miss your left turn onto the gravel road. Your landmarks are a brown/white "Island Pond" sign and a green/white gate. After turning left onto the gravel road, proceed for 0.3 mile to the top of a small rise where Island Pond comes into view and the white-blazed A.T. crosses. Turn right onto the A.T. and continue below.

Return Trip: After descending for about 250 feet, the A.T. turns left on an old woods road, known as the Island Pond Road, at a small wetland. In another 450 feet, the A.T. turns right to climb Green Pond Mountain, but you should continue straight ahead on the unmarked Island Pond Road. You will be following Island Pond Road for the next 2.0 miles.

After paralleling the western shore of Island Pond for 0.6 mile, Island Pond Road bears left and is joined (from the right) by the inverted-red-triangle-on-white-blazed A-SB Trail. Continue downhill on Island Pond Road to a very wet area and the most difficult water crossing of the entire loop. Just beyond, keep right at the fork, following the A-SB Trail. In another 75 feet, turn right again and head south (uphill) on the co-aligned A-SB Trail and Island Pond Road. Note: Those wishing to explore this area further (there is an old cabin and a lakeside view nearby) should refer to Chapter 13.

For the remainder of your run back to Route 106 (Kanawauke Road), you continue straight ahead on Island Pond Road, which is well defined and offers a generally smooth running surface. Almost immediately, the A-SB Trail leaves to the left. At the top of a hill (at 4.0 miles on the shorter run, 6.0 miles on the longer run), the yellow-blazed Dunning Trail joins from the left. Note: The Boston Mine (described in Chapter 12) is 200 feet to the left along the Dunning Trail.

Proceed downhill on Island Pond Road. Soon, the Dunning Trail leaves to the right. Just beyond, the Nurian Trail joins briefly and then leaves to the left. Continue ahead on Island Pond Road, which climbs through mountain laurel and crests another hill – the eastern arm of Stahahe High Peak. After descending gently to moderately, Island Pond Road is joined from the left by the White Bar Trail at 4.8 miles (6.8 miles for the longer run). Continue ahead to Route 106, then turn left onto the paved road and follow it for 500 feet to the parking area, on the right, where the hike began. ★

Chapter 31   Lake Wanoksink

Type:	**Trail run or walk**
Distance:	**7.05 miles (2.2 miles are not intended to be run) or 9.05 miles (all runable)**
Attractions:	**Scenic lakes and wetlands, relatively good footing, solitude**
Lowest Elevation:	**775 feet**
Highest Elevation:	**1,190 feet**
Total Elevation Gain:	**1,220 feet (shorter hike) or 1,020 feet (longer hike)**
Parking GPS Coordinates:	**41.19850, -74.12950**
Map:	**NY-NJ TC Southern Harriman-Bear Mountain Trails – Map #118**

These two runs or walks are designed for persons with good "woods sense" (meaning that one is comfortable following unmarked roads and trails). In warm weather, insect repellent and a portable hydration device are essential. Three of the park roads used on these runs have confusingly similar names: Pine Meadow Road, Pine Meadow Road East, and Pine Meadow Road West. They are maintained by the Park (not by the New York-New Jersey Trail Conference). Be alert for rough, eroded stretches, especially on the ascents and descents. Runners are advised to explore the route carefully the first time out, becoming familiar with critical turning points and rough patches.

Access: Take N.J. Route 17 north to the New York State Thruway and take the first exit, Exit 15A (Sloatsburg). Turn left at the bottom of the ramp onto N.Y. Route 17 north and continue through the village of Sloatsburg. Just beyond the village, turn right at the next traffic light, following the signs for Seven Lakes Drive and Harriman State Park. Continue along Seven Lakes Drive for 4.4 miles, and turn left into the driveway for the Lake Sebago Boat Launch. Make a quick right and park in the lot just to the left of a green dumpster.

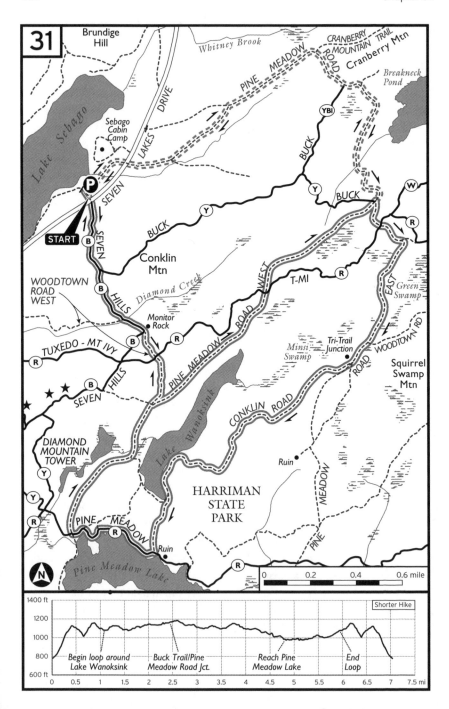

Description: Shorter run (begins with access hike, 1.1 miles): To access the run, begin by walking back up to Seven Lakes Drive. Across the road, you will notice the trailhead of the Seven Hills Trail, marked by three blue-on-white blazes. Follow the Seven Hills Trail uphill into the woods. In 0.35 mile, you'll pass the trailhead of the yellow-blazed Buck Trail on your left. In another 0.25 mile, you'll begin to follow a woods road (Woodtown Road West), which joins from the right, and you'll cross Diamond Creek. In another 500 feet, the Seven Hills Trail turns off to the right, but you will instead continue straight ahead on the unmarked Woodtown Road West. In another 0.35 mile, after crossing the red-dash-on-white-blazed Tuxedo-Mt. Ivy Trail, you will come to Pine Meadow Road West, a better-maintained road than the one you have been following.

Turn sharply left (northeast) on Pine Meadow Road West to begin your clockwise running loop around Lake Wanoksink. Note: You should carefully note this junction and surrounding landmarks, so you can easily identify it again at the end of your run. You might want to mark the junction with sticks or rocks.

Although Pine Meadow Road West is unmarked, it is a cross-country ski route, and you may notice some occasional cross-country ski markers. At 0.65 mile from the start of your run, the red-dash-on-white-blazed Tuxedo-Mt. Ivy Trail crosses. Then, at 1.35 miles, you'll reach a major intersection. Pay close attention here: The yellow-blazed Buck Trail goes off to the left, the unmarked Pine Meadow Road proceeds straight ahead, and Pine Meadow Road East (also unmarked) goes right.

Turn right onto Pine Meadow Road East and head uphill. In 500 feet, you'll once more cross the red-dash-on-white-blazed Tuxedo-Mt. Ivy Trail, and you'll make a rocky descent past a wet area. In another 0.65 mile, a woods road joins from your left, and 500 feet beyond, you'll reach a three-pronged fork in the road known as Tri-Trail Junction. Take the right fork.

Along Pine Meadow Road East

DAN BALOGH

You are now following the Conklin Road (also unmarked), which climbs to a pleasant view of Minsi Swamp. Continue on Conklin Road for a little over a mile until you arrive at Lake Wanoksink (on your right). Follow along the shore until the road becomes submerged and disappears. Here, you'll have to turn left

Lake Wanoksink

and follow a single-track path south along the edge of the lake for a short distance. Soon, a path leads to the right, but you should continue straight ahead until you reach the end of Conklin Road at beautiful Pine Meadow Lake.

Here you should turn right onto the red-square-on-white-blazed Pine Meadow Trail. Note: For the next half mile, you will be following a single-track hiking trail; please use caution and yield to walkers. Begin by climbing past an old cellar hole, keeping the Pine Meadow Lake shoreline on your left. Soon, the trail forks and you should again keep to your left, following the red-square-on-white blazes. At 0.35 mile, you'll pass an unmarked path on your left (which leads a short distance out to a scenic point on the lake) and then an unmarked woods road on your right.

At 0.45 mile, you'll reach Pine Meadow Road West, an unmarked but well-maintained dirt road. Stop a moment and look to the left. You should see a bridge, confirming that you have indeed reached Pine Meadow Road West. So far, you have run a total of 4.15 miles.

Turn right (away from the bridge) onto Pine Meadow Road West, with occasional cross-country ski markers, which begins to ascend. In 0.45 mile, after passing a pretty cascade on your left, you'll cross the outlet of Lake Wanoksink on a stone bridge. After 0.7 mile on Pine Meadow Road West (4.85 miles total run), you will reach a junction with Woodtown Road West, which you may have marked at the beginning of your run with sticks and/or rocks. Here, the run ends.

Bear left onto unmarked Woodtown Road West and follow it uphill. The route should look familiar: you are returning on the same hiking route you used to access your run. In 0.25 mile, you'll cross the red-dash-on-white-blazed Tuxedo-Mt. Ivy Trail, and in another 0.1 mile, the blue-on-white-blazed Seven Hills Trail will join from the left. Continue straight ahead, following the blue-on-white blazes. They will lead you back over Diamond Creek, past the yellow-blazed Buck Trail on your right, and finally downhill and across Seven Lakes Drive to the boat launch parking area where your car awaits you.

Longer run: The run begins at the east side of the Lake Sebago Boat Launch parking lot at the brown-and-red signs marking the start of a cross-country ski trail (just to the left of a green dumpster). The trail leads through stands of wild roses and is sporadically marked with red, blue and green markers. Follow the trail across Seven Lakes Drive and into a hemlock and hardwood forest, crossing several small bridges. In 0.8 mile, turn right onto Pine Meadow Road, an unpaved but maintained road. The road climbs gradually for most of its length.

In another 0.4 mile, a woods road (named the Cranberry Mountain Trail) continues straight ahead, but you should bear right, continuing on Pine Meadow Road. In 0.2 mile, you'll pass a black-stripe-on-yellow-blazed trail (a branch of the Buck Trail) on your right. Proceed ahead on Pine Meadow Road for another 0.7 mile until you reach a fork in the road (2.1 miles from the start). On the right, you'll see the yellow-blazed Buck Trail and straight ahead, the ski route continues

DAN BALOGH

Lake Wanoksink

as Pine Meadow Road West. Do not take either of these routes. Rather, turn left and follow the unmarked Pine Meadow Road East uphill. You are now beginning a grand loop of almost five miles, clockwise around Lake Wanoksink.

In 500 feet, you'll cross the red-dash-on-white-blazed Tuxedo-Mt. Ivy Trail, and you'll make a rocky descent past a wet area. In another 0.65 mile, a woods road joins from your left, and 500 feet beyond, you'll reach a three-pronged fork in the road known as Tri-Trail Junction. Take the right fork.

You are now following Conklin Road (also unmarked) which climbs to a pleasant view of Minsi Swamp. Continue on Conklin Road for a little over a mile until you arrive at Lake Wanoksink (on your right). Follow the shore until the road becomes submerged and disappears. Here, you'll have to turn left and follow a single-track path south along the edge of the lake for a short distance. Soon, a path leads to the right, but you should continue straight ahead until you reach the end of Conklin Road at beautiful Pine Meadow Lake.

Here you should turn right onto the red-square-on-white-blazed Pine Meadow Trail. Note: For the next half mile, you will be following a single-track hiking trail; please use caution and yield to walkers. Begin by climbing past an old cellar hole, keeping the Pine Meadow Lake shoreline on your left. Soon, the trail forks and you should again keep to your left, following the red-square-on-white blazes. At 0.35 mile, you'll pass an unmarked path on your left (which leads a short distance out to a scenic point on the lake) and then an unmarked woods road on your right.

At 0.45 mile, you'll reach Pine Meadow Road West, an unmarked but well-maintained dirt road. Stop a moment and look to the left. You should see a bridge, confirming that you have indeed reached Pine Meadow Road West. So far, you have traveled a total of 4.9 miles.

Turn right (away from the bridge) onto Pine Meadow Road West, with occasional cross-country ski markers, which begins to ascend. You'll be following the road for the next two miles. Along the way, you'll pass a pretty cascade on your left, cross an outlet of Lake Wanoksink on a stone bridge, and, in 0.7 mile, pass unmarked Woodtown Road West on your left (keep right at this fork). After 1.35 miles on Pine Meadow Road West, the red-dash-on-white-blazed Tuxedo-Mt. Ivy Trail crosses. Proceed 0.7 mile further to the end of Pine Meadow Road West at a major intersection – the same intersection you reached earlier in your run. You have now completed the loop portion of your run. You've covered 6.95 miles so far and have 2.1 miles left to go.

DAN BALOGH

Stone bridge over the outlet of Lake Wanoksink along Pine Meadow Road West

To complete your run, continue straight ahead (not right) on Pine Meadow Road. If this looks familiar, it is because you are following the exact same route you began your run on, except in reverse. Continue to follow the main road, with occasional cross-country ski markers. The road is mostly downhill, which is a welcome change after all that climbing. At 7.85 miles, a woods road (the Cranberry Mountain Trail) goes off to the right, but you should bear left to continue on Pine Meadow Road. At 8.25 miles, the cross-country ski trail turns left at a rock cairn, leaving Pine Meadow Road. Turn left here, and follow the ski trail downhill through the woods and back over the wooden bridges. The trail soon turns right, ascends briefly, crosses Seven Lakes Drive, and leads back to your car at 9.05 miles.

Final note: If you prefer smoother terrain (for a strong finishing kick), the following variation is recommended. When you reach the rock cairn at 8.25 miles, do not turn left. Instead, continue straight ahead on Pine Meadow Road until it ends at Seven Lakes Drive. Then, simply turn left onto Seven Lakes Drive and follow it for 0.4 mile to the boat launch parking area (on your right) and your car. 🏃

Chapter 32   Second Reservoir

Type:	**Trail run or walk**
Distance:	**8.7 miles**
Attractions:	**Scenic lakes and wetlands, relatively good footing, solitude**
Lowest Elevation:	**775 feet**
Highest Elevation:	**1,190 feet**
Total Elevation Gain:	**1,000 feet**
Parking GPS Coordinates:	**41.19850, -74.12950**
Map:	**NY-NJ TC Southern Harriman- Bear Mountain Trails – Map #118**

Access: Take N.J. Route 17 north to the New York State Thruway and take the first exit, Exit 15A (Sloatsburg). Turn left at the bottom of the ramp onto N.Y. Route 17 north and continue through the village of Sloatsburg. Just beyond the village, turn right at the next traffic light, following the signs for Seven Lakes Drive and Harriman State Park. Continue along Seven Lakes Drive for 4.4 miles, and turn left into the driveway for the Lake Sebago Boat Launch. Make a quick right and park in the lot just to the left of a green dumpster.

Description: The route begins on the east side of the Lake Sebago Boat Launch parking lot, at the brown-and-red signs marking the start of a cross-country ski trail (just to the left of a green dumpster). The trail leads through stands of wild roses and is sporadically marked with red, blue and green markers. Follow the trail across Seven Lakes Drive and into a hemlock and hardwood forest, crossing several small bridges. In 0.8 mile, turn right onto Pine Meadow Road, an unpaved but maintained road. The road climbs gradually and,

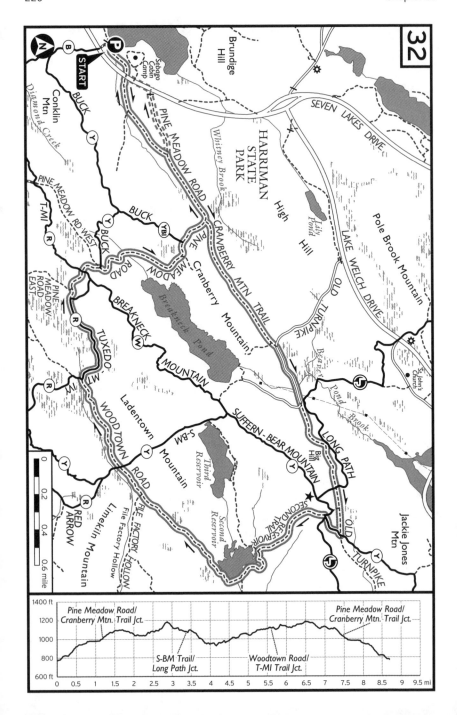

DAN BALOGH

Second Reservoir

in 0.4 mile, reaches a junction with the Cranberry Mountain Trail, a woods road which begins on the left. The junction is marked with an orange-red telephone cable sign on a wooden post.

Bear left and follow the Cranberry Mountain Trail straight ahead, along the foot of Cranberry Mountain. You're now following the route of a buried telephone cable line. Where the trail becomes wet or rough, you can usually find easier terrain on the extreme left or right side of the road. In 0.8 mile, continue straight past some orange blazes on your right. In another 200 feet, continue straight again, joining a paved road – the route of the Old Turnpike. In 0.3 mile, the paved road turns right, but you should – once again – proceed straight ahead to continue along the Old Turnpike (the route of the buried telephone cable line). Soon, you'll pass a metal sign inscribed "Foot Traffic Only."

In 0.6 mile, the aqua-blazed Long Path crosses. In another 0.25 mile (just beyond an orange-red telephone cable sign), watch closely for an intersection with the yellow-blazed Suffern-Bear Mountain (S-BM) Trail. Turn right at this junction onto the S-BM Trail and follow it south, along a woods road.

In 0.15 mile, the aqua-blazed Long Path joins from the left. Pay close attention, as just ahead, the S-BM Trail and Long Path both turn right, but you should continue straight ahead along the woods road (which is now unmarked).

The woods road, known as the Second Reservoir Trail, climbs briefly but soon begins a steady descent toward the Second Reservoir. The road is rather rough in places. At the water's edge (0.5 mile from where the S-BM Trail and Long Path split away), you will reach a T-intersection with a woods road that leads around the Second Reservoir. Turn left and follow along the edge of the reservoir, keeping the water on your right. Soon, you'll cross an outlet of the reservoir (use care; you may get your feet wet). Keep right and follow along the top of the dam. After crossing another outlet of the reservoir, you'll reach a T-intersection with the unmarked Woodtown Road. Here, you should turn right.

Woodtown Road parallels the Second Reservoir for a short distance, then continues its westward path through the quiet forest. Although unmarked, Woodtown Road is obvious and easy to follow. In 0.8 mile, continue straight ahead as another unmarked woods road (known as the File Factory Hollow Trail) goes off to the left. In another 0.15 mile, the yellow-blazed S-BM Trail crosses, and Woodtown Road begins a gentle ascent.

In another 0.55 mile (5.6 miles from the start), the red-dash-on-white-blazed Tuxedo-Mt. Ivy (T-MI) Trail comes in from the right. Turn right here, leaving Woodtown Road, and follow the T-MI Trail uphill on a narrower woods road. Note: If you miss this right turn, you will immediately reach a wooden footbridge. Turn around and retrace your steps; the junction is just a few steps back.

Outlet of Second Reservoir

Woodtown Road

The T-MI Trail follows a runable woods road through a pretty stretch of hardwoods and blueberry bushes. In 0.65 mile, the T-MI Trail turns right onto a narrow path (this junction is marked with a small rock cairn), but you should continue straight ahead on the woods road. Just ahead, you'll reach a T-intersection with a wide, well-travelled woods road (Pine Meadow Road East). Turn right onto the unmarked Pine Meadow Road East and in 0.1 mile, the T-MI Trail will cross. In another 0.1 mile, Pine Meadow Road West comes in from the left, and you should continue straight ahead, now following Pine Meadow Road.

Pine Meadow Road, with occasional cross-country ski markers, is mostly downhill, which is a welcome change after all that climbing. At 7.45 miles, the Cranberry Mountain Trail goes off to the right, but you should bear left to continue on Pine Meadow Road. You are now following the same route you followed at the start of your run, but in reverse, heading back to your car. At 7.9 miles, the cross-country ski trail turns left at a rock cairn, leaving Pine Meadow Road. Turn left here, and follow the ski trail downhill through the woods and back over the wooden bridges. The trail soon turns right, ascends briefly, crosses Seven Lakes Drive, and leads back to your car at 8.7 miles.

Final note: If you prefer smoother terrain (for a strong finishing kick), the following variation is recommended. When you reach the rock cairn at 7.9 miles, do not turn left. Instead, continue straight ahead on Pine Meadow Road until it ends at Seven Lakes Drive. Then, simply turn left onto Seven Lakes Drive and follow it for 0.4 mile to the boat launch parking area (on your right) and your car. 🏃

Chapter 33 Rockhouse Runabout

Type:	**Trail run or walk**
Distance:	**5.4 miles or 6.7 miles (with add-on)**
Attractions:	**Lake Askoti, Hasenclever Mine and a Civil War-era cemetery**
Lowest Elevation:	**890 feet**
Highest Elevation:	**1,180 feet**
Total Elevation Gain:	**850 feet or 1,040 feet (with add-on)**
Parking GPS Coordinates:	**41.24202, -74.10229**
Map:	**NY-NJ TC Northern Harriman-Bear Mountain Trails – Map #119**

Access: Take N.J. Route 17 north to the New York State Thruway and take the first exit, Exit 15A (Sloatsburg). Turn left at the bottom of the ramp onto N.Y. Route 17 north, and continue through the village of Sloatsburg. Just beyond the village, turn right at the next traffic light, following the signs for Seven Lakes Drive and Harriman State Park. Follow Seven Lakes Drive for 7.1 miles and proceed straight across Kanawauke Circle. Continue following Seven Lakes Drive for another 0.7 mile to the parking area for Lake Skannatati, on the left side of the road.

Description: Due to terrain and navigational considerations, you will need to walk 0.2 mile on an unmarked trail to reach the starting point of this run. At the southern end of the parking area, find the aqua blazes of the Long Path which lead uphill along a brook, across Seven Lakes Drive and to the southern tip of Lake Askoti. Here, the Long Path heads uphill to the right, but you should stay left, following a scant shoreline path along Lake Askoti and across an inlet of the lake. After 0.1 mile of nasty terrain, you will no longer be able to follow the shoreline. At this point, a woods road leads uphill and to the right. Begin your run here by following this unmarked but well-defined woods road.

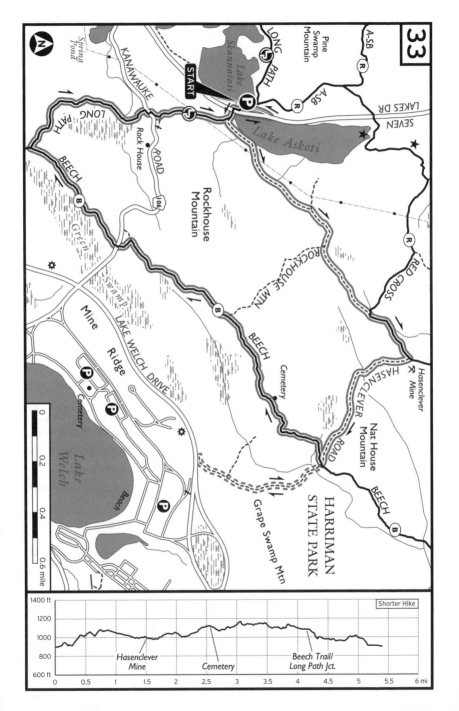

33

N

Spring Pond

LONG PATH

KANAWAUKE

Pine Swamp Mountain

Long Swamp Mountain

Lake Skannatati

A-SB

R

A-SB

R

SEVEN LAKES DR

START

P

LONG PATH

BEECH

B

Rock House

ROAD

106

Rockhouse Mountain

Lake Askoti

★

R

Green Swamp

Mine Ridge

LAKE WELCH DRIVE

B

ROCKHOUSE MTN

BEECH

RED CROSS

R

HASENCLEVER

Hasenclever Mine

☆

P

Cemetery

P

Lake Welch

Beech

☆

Cemetery

Nat House Mountain

ROAD

BEECH

B

P

Grape Swamp Mtn

HARRIMAN STATE PARK

Scale:
0
0.2
0.4
0.6 mile

Shorter Hike

1400 ft

1200

1000

800

600 ft

Hasenclever Mine

Cemetery

Beech Trail/ Long Path Jct.

0   0.5   1   1.5   2   2.5   3   3.5   4   4.5   5   5.5   6 mi

The woods road crosses a telephone line and makes a series of short climbs, then descends gradually. At 1.25 miles, you will be joined by the red-cross-on-white blazes of the Red Cross Trail. Continue descending gently on the woods road for another quarter mile to the Hasenclever Mine complex. There are several pits on the left and a flooded mine shaft on the right.

Turn right onto the unmarked Hasenclever Road, which was a county road until 1910. The road remains in relatively good condition, so you'll have smooth running for the next 0.65 mile. After crossing a small brook on a concrete bridge (with an interesting birch tree alongside the bridge), you'll begin a gradual climb up Nat House Mountain. Next, the road descends for about 0.1 mile to the blue-blazed Beech Trail. Keep a close eye out for this trail junction and turn right, following the blue blazes.

Note: If you wish to add a hill and another 1.3 miles to your run, do not turn right on the blue-blazed trail yet. Rather, continue straight on the unmarked Hasenclever Road. After crossing a small concrete bridge, you will climb about 100 feet over the next half mile. Hasenclever Road ends at a cut,

Concrete bridge on Hasenclever Road

just above Lake Welch Drive. Return as you came. Watch carefully for a blue blaze on your right and immediately turn left (west) to follow the blue-blazed Beech Trail.

After crossing a small brook, you will ascend gradually, crossing a field and passing by some thorny bushes. Continue climbing until you reach a Civil War-era cemetery at the top of a hill. Continue through mountain laurels and hardwoods, passing the unmarked Rockhouse Mountain Trail on your right at 3.0 miles (4.3 miles if you did the add-on). The trail passes below the summit of Rockhouse Mountain, then descends gradually and turns left before crossing the paved Route 106 (Kanawauke Road) at 3.6 miles (4.9 miles with the add-on). Continue for another 0.6 mile, passing above a pretty evergreen-lined swamp, until you reach the end of the Beech Trail. Turn right here, now following the aqua-blazed Long Path. Portions of this rocky trail may difficult to run. The Long Path descends to a phragmites-filled wetland, crosses its outlet by a stand of pine trees, then turns right onto Route 106. It follows the road for about 250 feet, then turns left and reenters the woods.

For the last half mile of the hike, follow the Long Path over a small rise, cross a telephone line, and descend to Seven Lakes Drive. Turn right now and follow Seven Lakes Drive north for 0.1 mile. Watch for cars as you make a sharp left and descend on the pavement to your car. 🏃

Civil War-era cemetery on the Beech Trail

Chapter 34 **Horn Hill Bike Path**

Type:	**Mountain bike, trail run or walk**
Attractions:	**Only bike trail in Harriman-Bear Mountain, evergreen forest, streams. Short distance and close proximity to parking area are favorable for beginners.**

Shorter Loop

Distance:	**3.85 miles**
Lowest Elevation:	**475 feet**
Highest Elevation:	**735 feet**
Total Elevation Gain:	**400 feet**

Longer (figure-8) Loop

Distance:	**5.6 miles**
Lowest Elevation:	**475 feet**
Highest Elevation:	**885 feet**
Total Elevation Gain:	**670 feet**
Parking GPS Coordinates:	**41.28866, -74.02306**
Map:	**NY-NJ TC Northern Harriman-Bear Mountain Trails – Map #119**

For its entire length, this hike follows the Horn Hill Bike Path – the only trail in Harriman State Park that is open to mountain bikes. Although it has been officially designated as a bike trail, its usage by cyclists is rather sparse, and it is an excellent route for running or hiking.

Before beginning your trip, take a good look at the map. Both the longer and shorter loops are marked as one-way routes. The longer loop makes a figure-eight pattern. At the center of this figure eight, the two loops are co-aligned for 0.1 mile. Thus, you will cover this short trail section twice if you choose to do the longer loop.

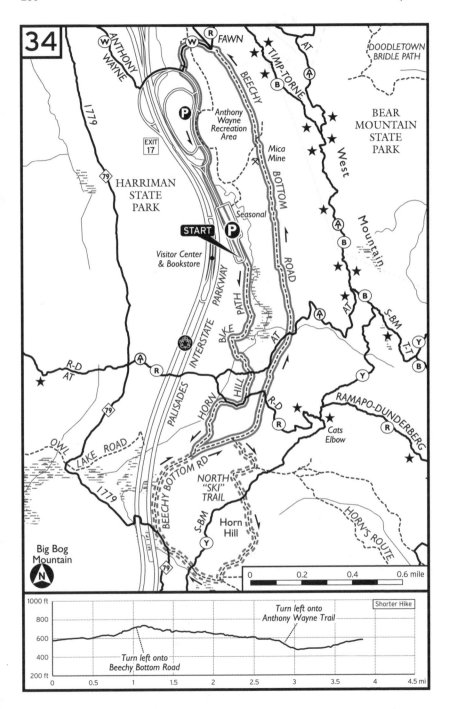

Access: Take the Palisades Interstate Parkway to Exit 17 (Anthony Wayne Recreation Area), which is three miles southwest of the Bear Mountain Bridge. Proceed past the first parking lot, then turn left at a sign for the "Far South Parking Lot," continue through this very large parking lot, and park at the southern end of the lot, near a kiosk and picnic benches. *Note:* If the south parking lot is closed to vehicles, you can park in the north lot and begin your run, ride or walk by following the above directions to the kiosk.

Description: From the kiosk at the southern end of the parking area, proceed south on the Horn Hill Bike Path, with blue-on-white diamond blazes, entering a white pine forest. The path is wide and level, but it is winding and there are many exposed tree roots. At 0.2 mile, you'll cross a short wooden bridge (the first of four). At 0.4 mile, the trail turns sharply left and crosses a longer bridge, and a short distance beyond, it crosses a bridge over Beechy Bottom Brook. After crossing a fourth bridge, you'll pass a small knoll on the left and continue across the white-blazed Appalachian Trail. There is a wooden sign at this intersection.

In another 0.1 mile, the red-dot-on-white-blazed Ramapo-Dunderberg (R-D) Trail joins from the left. After crossing two culverts, the R-D Trail leaves to the right. In another 0.2 mile, the Bike Path swings left and, at 1.05 miles, it reaches a wide woods road known as Beechy Bottom Road. Turn left onto Beechy Bottom Road.

Shorter loop: In 0.1 mile, another woods road bears right, but you should keep to the left, continuing on Beechy Bottom Road. If the leaves are down, you can see West Mountain towering ahead of you, through the trees. Skip ahead now to the section marked "Return Trip."

Longer loop: In 0.1 mile, turn right onto a woods road known as the North "Ski" Trail. In another 0.15 mile, turn sharply right and head uphill on a rocky woods road. After 0.15 mile of steep climbing, the trail descends slightly, crosses the yellow-blazed Suffern-Bear Mountain Trail, and climbs slightly. You have now traveled 1.5 miles.

Be careful as the rocky trail now heads downhill on a relatively steep grade. At 2.05 miles, you'll reach a T-intersection with Beechy Bottom Road. Note: There is a small Rockland County highway monument here, a remnant from the time when this was an official county road that connected Bulsontown and Queensboro. Turn right at this intersection. You will be following Beechy Bottom Road for the next 2.55 miles.

Soon, the yellow-blazed Suffern-Bear Mountain Trail crosses again and, in another 500 feet, the 1779 Trail (blue 1779 on white) joins from the left. The 1779 Trail runs jointly with the Bike Path for only 400 feet and then leaves to the left. Continue to follow the Bike Path along Beechy Bottom Road, with the Palisades Interstate Parkway on your left. The Bike Path climbs over a knoll and then follows a more level route. At 2.8 miles, notice that the first section of the bike path joins from the left (you were here previously, at the 1.05-mile point of your trip).

Continue straight ahead, and after 0.1 mile of familiar terrain (this is the center of the "figure-eight" loop), you will once again reach the woods road known as the North "Ski" Trail. This time, however, do not turn right on the North "Ski" Trail; instead, bear left and continue on the more level Beechy Bottom Road. You have traveled a total of 2.95 miles so far. Continue below in the section entitled "Return Trip."

Return trip: Continue along Beechy Bottom Road. You'll find the going to be quite easy in dry conditions, but sections of this road are prone to flooding, and the road can become very icy in the winter. In 0.25 mile, the red-dot-on-white-blazed Ramapo-Dunderberg Trail crosses, and in another 0.25 mile, the white-blazed Appalachian Trail crosses.

Runners along the Horn Hill Bike Path

DAN BALOGH

Hiker along Beechy Bottom Road

At 2.45 miles (shorter loop) or 4.2 miles (longer loop), you'll reach a T-intersection. Here, you should turn right. Just beyond, a side road leads uphill to the right, but you should bear left, continuing on the wide, level Beechy Bottom Road. Soon, a black metal pipe comes in from the right and begins to run along the road. About 0.4 mile beyond the T-intersection, follow the Bike Path markers as the Bike Path turns left, leaving Beechy Bottom Road, and begins to descend on a gravel park road. The Bike Path is now coaligned with the white-blazed Anthony Wayne Trail. After crossing another park road, the road you are following curves to the left and ends at a locked gate at the paved entrance road to the Anthony Wayne Recreation Area. This is the same road you drove on when you entered the area. You have now reached the end of the Horn Hill Bike Path.

Turn left onto the paved entrance road and proceed past the huge north parking lot. (If you parked here, you will find your car on the right.) Just beyond the lot, the road curves to the right to merge onto the Palisades Interstate Parkway, but you should turn left toward the south parking lot. Continue straight ahead (south) across the parking lot until you reach your car, near the kiosk where you began your trip. ✟

Chapter 35 **Doodletown Bridle Path**

Type:	**Cross-country ski, trail run or walk**
Distance:	**5.25 miles**
Attractions:	**Historic roads, scenic valleys, Doodletown Reservoir**
Lowest Elevation:	**175 feet**
Highest Elevation:	**715 feet**
Total Elevation Gain:	**955 feet**
Parking GPS Coordinates:	**41.30414, -74.01601**
Map:	**NY-NJ TC Northern Harriman-Bear Mountain Trails – Map #119**

The scenic Doodletown Bridle Path was first opened to the public as a horse and ski trail in 1935. Nestled between Bear and Dunderberg Mountains, it circles the historic former hamlet of Doodletown. Although Doodletown has been unoccupied since 1965, the valley in which it is located was first settled as far back as 1762. While most of the Bridle Path is in good condition, runners and skiers should note that there are a few badly eroded and wet sections. Note that this hike accesses the Bridle Path loop from the west (not from Bear Mountain's South Parking Area, where the horses were originally stabled).

Access: Take the Palisades Interstate Parkway north to Exit 19. Turn right onto Seven Lakes Drive, continue for 0.5 mile, and turn right onto an unmarked paved road that leads in a short distance to a parking area. (This is the first right turn you'll come to on Seven Lakes Drive.)

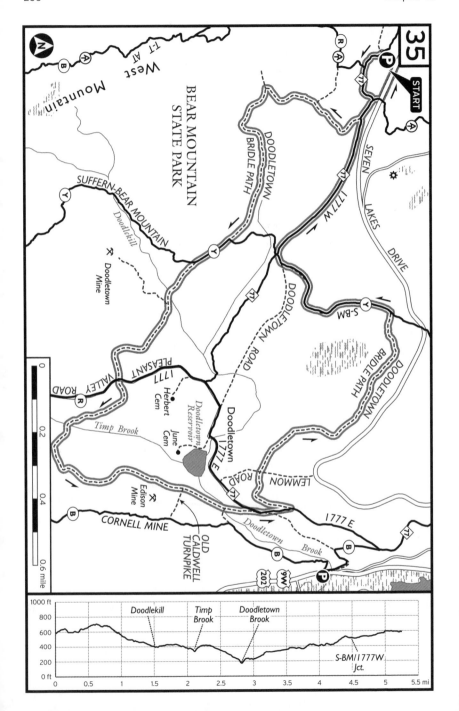

Along the Doodletown Bridle Path

Description: On the left (east) side of the parking area, you'll notice a white circular blaze with a red 1777W. Follow this trail uphill into the woods. In a short distance, the white-blazed Appalachian Trail (A.T.) joins from the right. Continue straight ahead, now following both white and 1777W blazes. About 0.2 mile from the start, the trails turn left and descend steeply for a short distance. At the base of the descent, the white A.T. blazes turn left and cross Seven Lakes Drive, but you should turn right and continue along the 1777W Trail, which follows a wide woods road. Watch carefully for a junction in 250 feet. Here, you should turn right onto the unmarked Doodletown Bridle Path. This is the start of a 4.75-mile loop on the Bridle Path, which you will be following in a counterclockwise direction.

Bridle Path Loop: Follow the Bridle Path uphill into the woods. In about 0.4 mile, you'll reach elevation 715 feet, which is the highest elevation of your trip. Here, the Bridle Path bears left at a T-intersection and soon begins a long descent, with a stream cascading through the valley on your left. Runners should take care, as some sections of the descent may be too eroded to run safely. As the Bridle Path levels off at 1.2 miles, the yellow-blazed Suffern-Bear Mountain Trail joins from the left. In another 750 feet, the Suffern-Bear Mountain Trail leaves to the right. The Bridle Path crosses the Doodlekill on rocks at 1.5 miles, and in another 0.35 mile, it crosses the wide Pleasant Valley Road (the route of the 1777 Trail).

The Bridle Path now descends to cross Timp Brook on a culvert, with an attractive cascade on the right. It climbs briefly, curves to the left, and soon begins a steady descent. At 2.7 miles, it crosses a woods road known

as the Old Caldwell Turnpike (there is an historical marker at the junction). Here, there is a view of the Doodletown Reservoir (built in 1975) on the left. Then, at 2.85 miles, the Bridle Path crosses Doodletown Brook, below the reservoir dam, on a concrete bridge, with a picturesque gorge below on the right. In another 0.1 mile, the Bridle Path turns right onto an old paved road, the route of the 1777E Trail (red 1777E on white).

In 100 feet, you'll come to a fork. Bear left here, leaving the paved road, and follow the 1777E Trail uphill. At the next junction (marked by a large number "2"), make a sharp left onto another woods road, leaving the 1777E Trail. The Bridle Path climbs gradually, passing a marker commemorating the location of the First June Cemetery on the right and a limited view over the Hudson River and Dunderberg Mountain on the left. A short distance beyond, the Bridle Path crosses Lemmon Road at a sign for the "Doodletown Walking Tour." You have now traveled 3.25 miles.

The Bridle Path now climbs very gradually and soon begins to parallel Seven Lakes Drive (above on the right). Then, at 4.0 miles, as the Bridle Path curves to the left, the yellow-blazed Suffern-Bear Mountain Trail joins from the right. The Bridle Path now levels off. It soon resumes its climb, then descends and turns right onto a woods road (Doodletown Road). In 150 feet, as the road curves to the right, the yellow blazes leave to the left, but you should continue ahead on the woods road, now following the blazes of the 1777W Trail. The Bridle Path now begins a gentle climb, and some sections may be wet or rough. After closely paralleling Seven Lakes Drive (above on the right), you'll reach the spot where you began your 4.75-mile loop. You have now traveled a total of five miles. Unless you are planning to run the Bridle Path loop twice, you should skip ahead now to the section marked "Return Trip."

Doodletown Reservoir

Note: If you choose to run the Bridle Path loop a second time, you should turn left here (uphill). Continue by following the "Bridle Path Loop" directions once more. Running the Bridle Path Loop twice increases your total distance to 10 miles.

Return trip: Bear right and continue along the 1777W Trail. Soon, you'll reach an intersection with the white-blazed A.T. Turn right, follow the A.T. a short distance to Seven Lakes Drive, then turn left onto Seven Lakes Drive and follow it for 0.1 mile to the first left – an unmarked paved road which leads a short distance to the parking area where you began the hike. 🏃

Index

Other Hiking Books Available From the Trail Conference!

Authoritative Hiking Maps and Books by the Volunteers Who Maintain the Trails

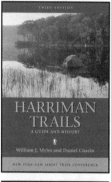

HARRIMAN TRAILS
Third Edition (2010), William J. Myles and Daniel Chazin
Bill Myles' original guidebook to the trails in Harriman-Bear Mountain State Parks has been completely revised by Daniel Chazin. It is much more than a guide – years of research have produced a fine history as well. Marked and unmarked trails, lakes, roads and mines are all covered in depth. A complete reference work, with many historical photos.
sc. 421 p. 5 3/8 x 8 1/8, B&W photos

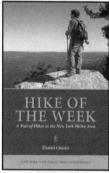

HIKE OF THE WEEK
First Edition (2013), Daniel Chazin
A selection of 52 hikes in the New York metropolitan area – one for each week of the year. The hikes are taken from Dan Chazin's popular *Hike of the Week* column in *The Record,* and are organized by season and level of difficulty. Each hike is accompanied by a map and a sidebar that focuses on some interesting aspect of the hike, such as history, geology, wildlife, etc.
sc. 358 p. 5 3/8 x 8 1/8, B&W photos and maps.

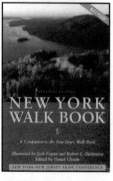

NEW YORK WALK BOOK
Seventh Edition (2005), Edited by Daniel Chazin
Illustrations by Jack Fagan and Robert L. Dickinson
"Indispensable reference to trails in New York State from Long Island to Albany. The hikers' 'Bible' since 1923."
The New York Times, 10/26/2001. Includes comprehensive trail descriptions, color maps, and information on ecology, geology and history.
sc. 484 p. 5 3/8 x 8 1/8, B&W photos and maps.

Visit www.nynjtc.org – more information and newest products!